Catching People in the Love Net

by
Bernard Williams

R.H. Boyd
Publishing
CORPORATION
A GLOBAL NAME IN PUBLISHING FOR OVER 100 YEARS

Nashville, Tennessee

Catching People in the Love Net
Bernard Williams

R.H. Boyd Publishing Corporation
6717 Centennial Boulevard
Nashville, Tennessee 37219

ISBN: _____

Printed in the United States of America

CONTENTS

SECTION III — CHRISTIAN RIGHTEOUSNESS

SECTION IV — LIVING IN HOPE AND TRUST

Then Jesus said to Simon,
"Do not be afraid;
from now on you will be catching people."
(Luke 5:10b, NRSV)

For by the grace given me I say to every one of you:
Do not think of yourself more highly than you ought,
but rather think of yourself with sober judgment, in
accordance with the measure of faith God has given you.
(Romans 12:3, NIV)

"For God so loved the world that he gave his only son,
so that everyone who believes in him may not perish
but may have eternal life."
(John 3:16, NRSV)

Catching People in the Love Net

"Caught in the Love Net" is a phrase that deals with human salvation from sin. It expresses God's grace (charis) and love (agape) as the fundamental aspects of this salvation. God saves humanity from sin for no other reason but His gracious love for it. As such, salvation has some important aspects that those who are redeemed or saved must follow. First, there is the human need to heed God's call for repentance and turn to God in faith and obedience. That is, the word of God is proclaimed and solicits a response from its hearers. That response must be affirmative in terms of the forsaking of self and turning to God as Lord and Savior. Human sin, if not repulsed and isolated, destroys humanity and its relationship with God. But those who repent and express faith in God through Jesus Christ, secure for themselves a place in His love and fellowship. Hence, the phrase "Caught in the Love Net."

When we are wrapped and tied and tangled in God we become securely rooted in His presence, protected and sealed by His power, and the constant recipients of a joy that "passeth all understanding." John 3:16 says it all, "For God so loved the world that He gave His only Son that whoever believes in Him should not perish, but have life everlasting." In this one verse the entire gospel is proclaimed and explained. Again, it points to human participation, one must believe. "Believe" as used here is more than a mere expression of going along with something, it is intended by the Johannine writer as a continuous action caused by a deep conviction that something is real and true. Thus, repentance is the initial step of one acting upon his or her belief that Jesus, as the Son of God, is come to set humanity in a right relationship with God (justification). This continuous belief involves living a life that is pleasing to God. It takes into consideration that one must go beyond the initial steps of believing and make a commitment to practice. One's work on a continuous basis becomes evidence of one's belief. Those who are securely caught in God's love net are those who live as Paul says, "in the Spirit" and "by the Spirit." As a resource for staying firmly entrenched in the Spirit, God's word motivates us to accept His precious gift of salvation through His Son Jesus Christ.

The intent and purpose of this book is to provide biblical and theological enrichment so that all who read and study its content will have a deeper understanding of God's love for them and develop a closer relationship with Him. These lessons, or textual discussions, are meant to enlighten Christians and others and open up opportunities for discussion and further study. Individuals and Bible study groups alike will find this resource useful as they ask, "How do I develop and maintain a healthy walk with my Creator and Benefactor?" The eighteen study lessons examine various passages of scripture that revolve around the theme of being caught in the love net, in four related aspects: proclamation and repentance, life in the Spirit, Christian righteousness, and living in hope and trust.

The first section of this study deals with the proclamation of the Gospel and the human response to it. God's love is thrown out as a love net, as a life-line for all to come to Him in repentance and faith. These four study lessons from Joel 1-2, Mark 2, 4-5, and Romans 10 provide the basic foundation of the Christian mission and purpose—namely God's salvation.

The second section of the study focuses on how we are to live after we have responded positively to God's divine initiative. God calls us out of the bondage of sin to experience His glorious freedom. This freedom is the actualization of the Sprit of God within us, the Apostle Paul's calls to freedom, to live the Gospel by way of the Sprit of God. We examine five passages of scripture, from Galatians and Romans, to find a biblical and theological basis for our new life in the love net.

The third section is actually a continuation of life in the Spirit covered in section two. It differs from section two, however in that it details Christian responsibility; Christians caught in the love net must make a deliberate effort to achieve God's standard of righteousness and live as a just and harmonious society. Selected scriptural text from Psalms 1 and 19, Psalms 82 and 113, Jeremiah, Romans 14, and Galatians 3 provide the foundation for the study.

The fourth and final section includes study from four different scriptures: Psalms 23 and 121, Psalm 42, Mark 6, and Psalm 78. The purpose of this group of lessons is to help Christians as they live to keep their hope, faith, and trust in God. They are also encouraged to "keep on keeping on," in the midst of rejection and ridicule. Christians are then directed to focus on their mission and pass their faith on to succeeding generations. When they fulfill their purpose they not only secure their own salvation, but they also secure the salvation of those who hear them.

This study is for the enlightenment of pastors, teachers, church workers, individual Christians, church groups, and others who want to study the scriptures more intently and use them as a basis for victorious living. *"Catching People in the Love Net"* has an evangelistic flavor that calls people to salvation, responsibility, and purpose. As a resource book for spiritual enrichment, this book and its author owe a great indebtedness to God, who sent Jesus Christ so that believers might be saved (in the love net) and have eternal life.

Section I

God's Call
To Repentance

Chapter One

Call to Repentance

— Joel 1–2 —

"God Wants You Back"

Return to me with all your heart, with fasting, with weeping, and with mourning; rend your hearts and not your clothing. Return to the Lord, your God, for he is gracious and merciful, slow to anger, and abounding in steadfast love, and relents from punishing (Joel 2:12-13, NRSV).

INTRODUCTION

God warns that He will judge His people. His judgment is a terrible one upon those who transgress against His will. The only way of escape is to repent by turning back to God, who offers forgiveness and restoration through His Spirit. This chapter investigates the need for people to repent for their sins. Failure to listen by obeying God's Word is an open path to experience his terrible judgment. Although the actual place of this event is unknown, it takes place during the post-exilic period. The book is seen as a transition from the Old Testament period to the New Testament. The pouring out of the Spirit of God upon all flesh and the call to repent and receive it are prominent New Testament themes that have their genesis in the Old Testament story of Israel's rebellion.

GOD'S WARNING

The land of Judah was devastated by locusts, which, like a huge army, had destroyed much of the vegetation in the land. A severe drought had only made a bad situation worse. Although the people of Judah had endured other tragedies, this one seemed to rank high among them. Both human beings and animals alike were suffering.

Amid this devastation and tragedy, the Lord called a citizen of Judah to provide a proper interpretation of the terrible events and to recommend a course of action for the people to follow.

The Book of Joel has two major concerns. It addresses the people, whose immediate crop supply is threatened by locusts. This threat affects the supply for over a year. However, as God's prophet, Joel understands that the people's problem is primarily a theological matter rather than a natural disaster. He interpreted the natural chaos upon Judah as God's judgment against them because of their sin and unfaithfulness. Joel describes the storm of locusts that devastated the land. They have stripped clean the vegetation and crops, and even hindered the work of the priests because of the lack of corn, wine, and oil to make holy offerings. Joel calls upon the priest to summon the people to a massive and urgent prayer meeting to bring about an end to this plague.

It is this calamity in which the prophet sees an even greater danger. Joel sees in this present emergency a more serious danger lurking in the horizon—the coming of the day of the Lord. It is the coming of the Lord and Israel's response to it, that is the major concern of this lesson. The locusts then become representative of the coming day of the Lord, a day of devastating judgment. The Edomites failed to take into consideration the day of the Lord, the day when God would judge His people in light of their defiance of Him. Joel sees, for the people of Israel, a similar day of impending judgment. Joel's vision here reminds one of Amos' "day of the Lord." Amos 5:18-20 reveals the day of the Lord as likened unto one who escapes from a lion only to run into a bear, or one who leans on a wall only to be bitten by a snake. There is no escape from the judgment of God. Therefore, Joel warns them to return to the Lord and petition Him for forgiveness and mercy. Joel holds out hope, but only if the people repent and seek God with prayer and fasting. He strongly encouraged all the people of Judah to return to God in genuine faith and to seek His grace and mercy.

The Book of Joel is the second of the prophetic books grouped in the section known as Minor Prophets, which concludes the Old Testament. The book does not provide any clear details concerning the date, place, and time of its composition. Its message, however, clearly expresses timeless significance. In this chapter, which generally warns of impending divine judgment, three things are further emphasized: the announcement of the coming of God's army (2:1-2); the call to return to the will of the Lord (vv. 12-13); and the pouring out of the Spirit of God (vv. 28-32). These three sections emphasize the call to repentance and God's response to repentance.

The people of Israel and Judah were known for their general disregard for the prophets of the Lord, either by ignoring or failing to comply. Joel is rare among the prophets in that apparently the people heeded his words. They do not fail to take the opportunity to secure themselves in his love net

THE COMING OF GOD'S ARMY—HIS JUDGMENT (JOEL 2:1-2)

The name Joel means, "Yahweh (the Lord) is God." His name is appropriate to his task. The prophet, identified as the son of Pethuel, announces boldly and with forcefulness the power of Yahweh as God. This word encompasses the people of Joel's day, but according to Joel 1:3, it is a word for those of generations to come. That word is the coming of God to judge His people. Joel 2:1 begins with the imperatives "Blow the trumpet" and "Sound the alarm." Why? Because the day of the Lord is coming, it is very near. It is no joking matter, nor one to be taken lightly. The Edomites experienced the day of the Lord, and it was a matter that they would rather not have experienced. Joel describes this day of the Lord in much of the same way that Amos describes it, as a day of darkness (Amos 5:20).

It is not only a day of darkness and gloominess, but it is a day wherein the sun cannot be seen or observed because of the thickness of the clouds prohibiting light from seeping through. What remains of verse two has to be taken in conjunction with verse 11. The people that come forth in verse 2 are described in verse 11 as the "army of the Lord." This army comes to defend the integrity of a righteous God, to execute His judgment. Thus, the call in verse 1 is actually a warning that His judgment is on the way. The blowing trumpet or horn, coupled with darkness and trembling people, is a portrait of the awesome power facing Jerusalem. The judgment of God comes not in silence but in public acclaim as befitting His divine royalty.

CALL TO REPENTANCE
(JOEL 2:12-13)

The prophet admonishes the people that God desires and requires their whole heart, and includes fasting, weeping, and mourning. These actions are the usual expressions of repentance for Israel. Tearing (rend) garments was usually a sign of grief. God is not interested in torn clothing and outward signs. The Lord wants a torn, repentant heart. In Hebrew psychology, the heart is the seat of the will, even more than one's affections. In this passage the Lord calls for double repentance. The Lord will repent when His people repent. He will turn from His intentions as announced, He will respond to the people as persons, and He will change His plan of action from judgment to mercy. When we turn to God He turns to us.

God does not come to ambush His people, nor does He come purposefully to catch them in their sin. The imperatives to blow the trumpet and to sound the alarm are actually warnings that the time has come to prepare for His coming judgment. The proper response to this divine warning is given in these verses. The question in verse 11, inquiring who can endure the judgment of God, beckons for an immediate response. No one! No one can stand the judgment of the holy and righteous one.

These verses (vv. 12-13) provide a startling contrast to the previous one. The greatness of God, in His thundering judgment, serves to put His people on notice that there is an out; there is a way of escape. The shift from a description of God's vast army is emphasized in the use of the two adverbs, followed by a short imperative: "Now therefore," saith the Lord, "Turn to me with all your heart with fasting, with weeping, and with mourning." God wants His people to respond. God Himself appeals to His people and encourages their repentance. The word "turn" has great significance here. It applies not only to the people, but to God as well. It is used both in verses 12 and 13, in relationship to Israel's turning to God, and in verse 14 regarding God turning to them. The implication is that if they return to God, He will turn from the course of His wrath and impending judgment.

The people had expected salvation to come from the Lord, but He would bring judgment instead. But the people still have hope in that the judgment is not necessary. They have an option to repent and change the course of action. The writer defines turn as change, a change on the part of those being judged. It is a change of direction, a change away from hopelessness to a change to something better. He calls for a change or turn from sin to God and His righteousness. Their change toward God provokes a change in the judgment of God. This change is a change of heart, a change of a person's thoughts and actions. This type of change, according to the writer, carries with it the connotation of sorrow and sacrifice. Repentance is godly sorrow that we have hurt God, others, and ourselves. Turning toward God for change involves much more than participation in religious activity, the use of religious language, or the adorning of religious paraphernalia. God's desire for a changed heart is made clear in His message through the prophet Hosea when the people thought that their rituals were good enough to satisfy the Lord. "Not so," God says. "For I desired mercy, and not sacrifice; and the knowledge of God more than burnt offerings" (6:6, KJV).

Joel closes this section by reminding his audience of the divine characteristics of God: The Lord is gracious and merciful; He is slow to anger; kind and forgiving. In other words, if they renew their covenant with God, they will find a loving God who turns from His righteous judgment as an act of grace and mercy. Although one cannot dictate the response of the sovereign God, Joel emphasizes that human repentance is the first step to appeasing His wrath. God's desire to see His people living in a state of blessedness and not punishment and wrath is apparent here.

GOD WILL POUR OUT HIS SPIRIT (JOEL 2:28-29)

This section of the study conveys that God rewards repentance not only with physical restoration, but also with the pouring out of His Spirit upon Israel. The use of the possessive pronoun "my" indicates the sovereign will and claim of God upon Israel. The Spirit of God is the power behind all prophecy. His Spirit represents God's desire for all people to be agents of his revelation to the world. What a blessing to be made privy to the will of God! Joel prophesied of a day when the Lord's world would be shaken and everyone who calls on His name will be saved. In the New Testament, both Peter and

Paul taught the fulfillment of this prophecy in the coming of Christ and the outpouring of His Spirit at Pentecost. Acts 2: 21 affirms the fulfillment of this promise, "and it shall come to pass, that whosoever shall call on the name of the Lord shall be saved" (KJV).

These verses emphasize God's new method of communication with His people. It is communication where God manifests His will to all; the people shall prophesy, dream dreams, and see visions. God's word had not been communicated to the masses. He had spoken primarily through prophets, but now the Spirit of God makes known the will of God upon the human heart. God moves Israel to a new level and to a new relationship with Him, one where He will manifest Himself in the hearts of His people. These verses hold tremendous hope for all people. His marvelous Spirit would not be restricted to only a few. God's hope will extend to all persons without regard for age, gender, or social and economic barriers. They will all become as prophets, knowing God's will.

SUMMARY

This text calls upon us to acknowledge the coming of the judgment of God in our lives. All people must answer to God for their disobedience. God does not turn away from His people on His own accord. However, He cannot be turned toward persons who are turned away from Him. God calls His people to repentance and pleads for our return to Him. Repentance means to turn to God away from sin, to change our lives in accordance to His will. Although God in His sovereignty has the right to judge and punish us for our sin, we are reminded that He offers forgiveness and restoration. God's loving character expresses His gracious mercy and loving kindness. To those who are repentant, and who return to God, God promises to give His Spirit. He promises permanent communication with them. This Spirit empowers us to understand God's will for our lives and empowers us to keep it. The granting of His Spirit is God's seal of acceptance and approval stamped on the heart of all His people.

For Christians, God gave His Spirit at Pentecost and empowered the Church to proclaim the Gospel. By spreading the Gospel, we are fulfilling His command to catch people in the divine love net and securing our own salvation as well. The Gospel requires us to repent of our sins and to turn to God in faithful obedience. Those who hear the message and turn to God are reconciled to His fellowship, but divine judgment awaits those who reject it.

DISCUSSION QUESTIONS

1. Why does Joel call for human repentance?

2. When one considers the divine love net, what are some of the conditions by which one enters into the presence and security of God's presence?

3. How does the Spirit of God participate in human salvation?

4. What are the conditions for repentance?

5. Why does God choose to save us?

CHAPTER TWO

The Beginning of the Gospel

— Mark 2:3-12, 14-17 —

"Jesus Calls Sinners"

He (Jesus) said to them, "Those who are well have no need of a physician, but those who are sick; I have come to call not the righteous but sinners" (Mark 2:17, NRSV).

INTRODUCTION

Mark's gospel account is remarkable for its precision. In this gospel, Jesus does not mince words. He speaks plainly and sharply. He is often confronted with demon-possessed people, those who consider him as an unlearned and untrained religious imposter, and teachers of the law who dismiss him as someone usurping the power and authority of God. The heart of this study lay in the identity of Jesus and His mission (2:6c). Their question in 2:6c leads to Jesus' response in verses 10 and 11, and they become the backdrop to understanding His mission noted in Mark 2:17. An examination of this text will provide some interesting clues about Jesus and why He came.

AN IMPORTANT TRUTH
(MARK 2:3-12)

This text begins with an account of Jesus preaching. Word of His presence spread throughout Capernaum, and crowds gathered to hear Him speak. The human traffic jam prevented normal entry in the house where Jesus preached. Four men carrying a crippled man made an opening in the roof and lowered the paralyzed man through it. Jesus, astounded by their faith, forgave the sins of the paralyzed man. His statement prompted negative reaction by the teachers of the law who were present in the crowd.

These religious teachers knew the law and served as interpreters, even protectors of it. Upon hearing Jesus speak of forgiveness, the teachers of the law immediately questioned Jesus' "over zealousness" to put Himself in the position of God, because only God could forgive sin. Yet, Jesus does not flinch from taking this sacred position. They want to know two things: Why Jesus speaks the way He does, and why He assumes the position that only God can hold.

They ask intriguing questions: Why does this fellow talk like that, and who can forgive sins but God alone? In between these questions, Mark sandwiches their conclusion. "He is blaspheming!" Blasphemy is either denial of the reality of God or claims of divine status for one's self. It is a crime punishable by death (Lev. 24:16).

Their conclusions and last statement offer not only a sense of their expertise in the law and the high esteem to which they held it but also point to the closeness of their hearts to any possibility that Jesus was the Messiah of God. Additionally, their questions and perceived skepticism cast doubt as to the legitimacy of their presence and purpose there. Not only were they present, but also they had front row seats to observe first-hand the events as they occurred. Misplaced and evil motives sometimes lay behind religious work and religious activities

Mark does not provide the details of Jesus' sermon on this occasion, but he has already shown the consistency between Jesus' preaching, teaching, and healing in proclamation of the Kingdom calling for change and His teaching showing people a better way to God, coupled with His authoritive disposition as one who speaks for God. Thus, the second question of the teachers of the law leads directly to one of Mark's main points. "Who can forgive sins but God alone?" They have deduced the truth, and it escapes them. Jesus' claim here is not that of a priest who could pronounce God's forgiveness of sin upon repentance, restitution, and sacrifice (see Lev. 4:5; 6; 17:11). His implicit claim ranks much higher than that. No! Jesus does what God does. That pattern has already been established in Mark 1. Jesus healed a woman with a fever, exorcised a demon, healed a man with leprosy, and commanded the demon-possessed man to "shut up." Yet, Satan and his angels must proclaim the truth when confronted by the "Holy One" of God.

This question is of paramount importance for people who live today, virtually 2,000 years removed from their first century counterparts revealed in the text. "Can Jesus forgive sin?" Sin is defined as "missing the mark" that God set for humanity. The question then becomes, can Jesus remove the one thing that has come between God and humanity? It was something only God could do. Now here was this "itinerant preacher" claiming this special privilege, a claim too ludicrous for it to have any amount of validity.

But the proof of Jesus' claim comes as He duplicates the very activity of God. First, He reads their hearts and "irons out" their very thoughts (Mark 8:16; 12:15). He, like God, knows the inner recesses of the human heart. Mark contrasts the reading of the facial expressions with the reading of the heart. Jesus reads that which is not readily apparent to the human eye or to human discernment. But they miss this.

Jesus takes a more open approach. He challenges the lawyers with a question of His own. His question to them is a rhetorical device used by Him to cause them to consider the folly of their heart's question. His question to them is one of great theological significance: Which is easier? To forgive sin in a verbal utterance or to demonstrate it by providing empirical proof by virtue of His ability to enable the man to rise and walk. Hebrew theology held that a person's physical infirmities resulted as a consequence of their sin. In Jesus' rhetorical reply, He will kill two birds with one stone. He will, by making the man walk, demonstrate His ability to forgive sin. Additionally, by making the man walk, He completed the prophetic test that demanded that a prophet's words be fulfilled. Indeed, forgiveness of sin is accompanied by an act of forgiveness.

This text also recognizes that a thorough examination be done of the whole person and not just a partial analysis. Jesus looks at the man's physical, spiritual, and emotional state and determines that the root of his physical impairment lay in his spiritual depravation. He forgives the man's sins. Sin and its evil companion of guilt cripple human potential and stifle human growth. Mark's point here is not to emphasize why bad things happen to people (sinful or otherwise) but to show that Jesus has the authority to forgive sin and to do the work of God. The work of God is the work of healing, of reconciling the gap between God and humanity.

The miracles of Mark show that the healing power of God is the interruption of God onto the human scene in a new and vivid way. It changes the question from "can one forgive sins?" to "who is this that comes in the name of God bringing forgiveness, healing, and salvation?" It reverses the age-old idea of continued sinful infliction. God, in Jesus, inaugurates a new age, an age of restoration of the whole person. Restoration of the whole person begins with a right relationship with God. The miracle demonstrates God's love and grace as supremely directed to humanity to restore them to God. Jesus coming to the world is evidence that He cast out the divine love net of human restoration to divine favor. This fact will be demonstrated in Jesus' selection of a human sinner to His ministry.

A REVEALED TRUTH (MARK 2:14-17)

This section begins another scene which goes through Mark 3:6. It focuses on Jesus' general reception by the general population and by religious leaders. The tension between the two is startling to say the least. As news of Jesus' activities spread throughout the countryside, the responses are not monotonous. They are varied with extreme enthusiasm for Him on the one hand, countered by extreme skepticism, jealousy and repugnancy for Him on the other. It is a conflict narrative that provides Jesus the occasion to highlight the purpose of His mission and of His selection of helpers to aid in its fulfillment. Here, Mark returns to the discipleship story that he began in the previous chapter. The passage emphasizes Jesus' choice of a person for ministry and where to dine. It is Mark's rendition of Jesus dining with Zaccheus recorded in Luke's gospel.

Jesus' choice is significant because of who He chooses and it outlines the one God chooses as the focus to exemplify His redemptive purpose. Jesus chooses Levi, a tax collector. Tax collectors, called publicans in the King James Version of the Bible, were the most unlikely candidates for religious activity. They were deemed a dishonest lot whose lives were governed by their greed. Further, to side with the oppressor (the Roman government) by taking employment as a tax collector resulted in a double negative effect. Yet, Jesus is not deterred from selecting him. Nor is He deterred from selecting you. The high call of ministry not only goes out to the poor, but it includes them. In fact, His call for service, as noted in His selection of Levi, means that it is open to all (the poor and the affluent) and even to the perceived unrighteous.

He comes calling sinners to redemption and even uses them to call other sinners. It is a duplication of the divine initiative of God entering the human frame of reference to communicate with humanity. Here He sends other humans to do so. He calls the sinner to catch other sinners in His divine love net. In this call, there are no perceived conditions except the willingness to leave everything behind, including a life of sin. Levi abandons his post, making an even more radical break with his past than the other disciples because he can never again return to such a shoddy profession. From that point on, Jesus takes control and acts as host of the dinner. The term "host" alludes to the earlier emphasis on Jesus' authority. But here the connection with this passage and the previous text is on what Jesus does. In the previous text, He forgives sin. He does what God does. In this text, He befriends sinners, the very ones devoid of dignity and respect. Jesus' presence indicates a restoration of the divine and human fellowship that was broken when humanity chose to sin. The dinner is an indication that sin and its deadly consequences of death and enmity will no longer be able to separate the creator from the creature. Real forgiveness of sin and the power to restore wholeness came in Jesus Christ. Therefore, the celebration points to the eschatological future when the restoration of fellowship will be full and complete. Thus, the reason for the dinner is not a party or a feast but to establish credibility with a ragtime group of ungodly creatures in order to bring them under the grace of God.

SUMMARY

This text focuses on Jesus' ability to forgive sin and to call others to join Him in proclaiming the gospel of God's grace to humanity. The Gospel of Jesus is the good news that God is come in Him to restore the divine-human fellowship. God entered the human frame of reference as a real person placing important value on human life. So important is humanity's restoration to divine fellowship that Jesus employs other humans to join Him in the call of salvation. This call means those who answer it must be willing to break with the past and leave all to follow him. The good news is that those who follow him, who heed his call, are caught in the divine love net.

DISCUSSION QUESTIONS

1.   How does Mark's theme of forgiveness emphasize being caught in the divine love net?

2.   Why is it important for the people to understand that Jesus does what God does?

3.   Compare and contrast this text with your understanding of forgiveness and the authority and example of Jesus to forgive.

4.   How do the motives of the religious leaders and those of Jesus compare in this text?

5.   What does restoration to divine fellowship mean for Mark?

CHAPTER THREE

Proclaim the Gospel
— Romans 10:1, 3-10, 12-17 —
"Is There An Answer?"

And how are they to hear without someone to proclaim him [Christ]? And how are they to proclaim him unless they are sent? (Romans 10:14-15, NRSV)

INTRODUCTION

The topic for discussion today, asks the question "Is there an answer?" This passage of scripture replies with a resounding "Yes!" There is an answer for all of life's problems. It was human pride that led to the sin of disobedience by the first parents and subsequently has remained as one of the major problems facing humanity today, which in this passage is none other than inordinate self-love. The answers to life's difficulties have already been provided in the preaching and teaching of the good news of the resurrection of Jesus Christ. The gospel message is salvation to God through faith in Jesus Christ. In presenting this answer to his readers, Paul points out three important things to establish the fact of humanity's salvation and the relevance of Jesus Christ to it: Paul's concern for Israel's salvation, salvation comes through faith, which is belief in Jesus and confession, and Israel's failure to accept Christ—what God did in Jesus Christ—and her refusal to understand His plan of salvation.

A REASON FOR CONCERN
(ROMANS 10:1)

Paul begins this chapter by making known his desire and prayer for the salvation of Israel. Paul is concerned that his explanation (9:30-32) of Israel's stubbornness to pursue salvation through works—righteousness might be seen as his advocating the complete destruction of the Jewish people. Verse 1 demonstrates Paul's affection for his people and suggests that we ought to be concerned with the community where we live. It is a true saying that "charity starts at home." Paul's concern for Israel does not leave out others. This concern expressed in Paul's prayer for Israel's salvation leads to his explanation of their faith and thus to their impending restoration.

SALVATION COMES NOT THROUGH HUMAN PRIDE BUT THROUGH FAITH IN JESUS CHRIST (ROMANS 10:3-10)

These verses offer Paul's explanation for his prayer. They have sought to obtain life, namely the salvation of God, by establishing a righteousness, which they were powerless to establish. Thus they were ignorant of God's requirements, his provisions, and of their abilities. This ignorance points out Israel's deficit and lack of understanding which led to the rejection of submitting to and accepting the righteousness of God in Jesus Christ. In other words, they rejected the answer to life God had given them. They relied on themselves. Israel, in seeking to establish its own way to life, trusted in itself and became arrogant and self-centered. The people became their own god and therefore failed to provide the proper example of the way to salvation that God desired them to be to the other nations. Israel lacked spiritual insight to help determine and distinguish between what was true and what was false. We must recognize what is genuinely important and avoid confusing it with what is plausible, but of secondary significance.

Genuine spiritual insight must be distinguished from a "pious sentimentalism" which causes us to focus on our own actions, and from preoccupation with religious forms and customs, which falsely celebrate human achievements. Only God can empower us to make good choices. Second, their zeal was not the result of true knowledge. That is not to say that religious enthusiasm is not important because it is. God wants us to attend worship regularly and joyfully, to tell others about Him with enthusiasm (like we cheer for our favorite sports figure or celebrity) but He wants us to do it out of true knowledge. True knowledge of God is the result of genuine spiritual insight. It is the result of having an intimate relationship with God; it is more than conforming to a group of rules and regulations that we can recite proudly as a preschooler recites the alphabet. True knowledge comes from a relationship of dependence upon God. It is submitting to God as the creator, sustainer, and redeemer of all life. Therefore, reliance upon God becomes the essential content of those who profess to have true knowledge. Third, it is this type of knowledge that provides the basis for our zeal. We know that, without God, all life loses its purpose, that we cannot reach our God given potential, and cannot have eternal life. Thus knowledge provides order to our living; it balances our enthusiasm with a comprehensive outlook and firm grasp of the realities of life. Israel's zeal was nothing more than a blind attempt to find the way in the dark.

People who trust in drugs, alcohol, peers, in their own abilities, sports, looks, fancy automobiles, and physical beauty are repeating the sin of pride, which drove Adam and Eve out of paradise, and led to the failure of the Israelites to recognize God's offer of salvation. In other words, they refuse to get in the love net of divine salvation that God has provided to them to pull them out of their own destructive sin.

SALVATION COMES THROUGH JESUS CHRIST (ROMANS 10:12-17)

This passage presents a problem. The greatest problem that human kind has ever faced is the problem of human pride constantly urging us to substitute for God's method some

other alternative that does not challenge and repudiate us and our way of thinking. In verse 3, Paul recounts how God provided the essential gift of salvation. In verse 4 he announces that that gift was Jesus Christ, and not works of righteousness. They could have obtained the gift of God through faith. Faith here denotes two things, which must be taken together as one. It is believing in the death, burial, and resurrection of Jesus Christ, and confessing Jesus as the Lord of life.

Thus acknowledgement and belief in the resurrection are essential to human salvation. Human kind can never live so righteous that it can be saved on its own efforts and merits. Humanity needs God. God has provided this gift in the perfect example of Jesus Christ. In Jesus' death, burial, and resurrection, the Spirit of God has come to empower humanity to live out its true purpose and to become an example or beacon of light to others. In other words, salvation, the answer to the problem of human pride, is yours now. Paul assures us that salvation is ours because we are justified before God through faith in the Lord Jesus Christ. By accepting Him we are emancipated from sin and are reconciled to God.

Thus by faith, by believing in, and accepting Christ as Lord, believers are ushered into a new life, which enables them to rise above the trials and temptations which beset us. It frees us from bondage, guilt, and low living. The new life is the result of a new power. We are faced with the terrible strength of the forces which oppress us. Only a spiritual power, which is mightier still, can break their hold. That is the power available in Christ, and Paul shows us why it is that Christ is able to redeem us. He points to his divine nature and triumph over death. Jesus Christ is Lord. God has entered the human frame of reference to deliver us from all evil, even death. That is to say, God entered our world to deliver us from the slavery of evil and sin. He threw out the life so that we might be caught in the net of divine fellowship and love.

SUMMARY

This lesson affirms that there is an answer to every problem we face in life. That answer lies in our faith in the death, burial, and resurrection of Jesus Christ. You can find comfort, strength, and hope in his work. In Christ, God has overcome every obstacle that we can face. Faith in Him activates the power of the Holy Spirit in our lives. Through His assistance, our problems are dealt with in a way that provides us victory over them. The various things that youth face in this twenty-first century are more complex than those of previous generations. Drugs promiscuous sex, peer pressure, acceptance, broken homes and dysfunctional families, multiple examples of evil, crime, and war are just a few of the problems human beings experience on a daily basis. Yet the truth of the matter is a strong abiding faith in the power of God rescues us from the feeling of uselessness. The word of God proclaimed in Jesus Christ says our only way out is through our trust in Him.

DISCUSSION QUESTIONS

1. What is Paul's desire for Israel?

2. What did the Jews believe about salvation?

3. Why is salvation through Christ important for contemporary believers?

4. Why is it important for believers to continue to proclaim faith in Christ as the way to God?

5. Contrast being caught in the love net with human pride.

CHAPTER FOUR

The Power of Jesus

— Mark 4:36-41; 5:2-13 —

"Saved by His Love"

He woke up and rebuked the wind, and said to the sea, "Peace! Be still!" Then the wind ceased, and there was a dead calm (Mark 4:39, NRSV).

INTRODUCTION

When I was a boy, I was awestruck by the power of Superman. He could leap tall buildings in a single bound, move faster than a speeding bullet, and possessed more power than a locomotive. Superman had X-ray vision, and because he worked at a newspaper office, he stayed abreast of events that required his attention and superhuman ability. However, as I matured, I discovered that the concept of Superman was the epitome of fantasy. No one could fly, outrun a speeding bullet, or stop a powerful train. I became disenchanted when I learned that Superman was not a real person and only existed in the minds of people who needed to escape and be humored by a world of fantasy. I found that when the world needed Superman, he was nowhere to be found. The world still suffered from violence, hate, disasters, crime and social injustice with no red-caped crusader coming to the rescue. Yet, I heard about a carpenter who sacrificed himself for humanity. I heard how this man taught people to love instead of hate and gave his life on a cross. I heard how this carpenter rebuilt lives and provided inner and spiritual resources for people to overcome their problems, seek his guidance to discover life's true purpose,

and to spread the message of God's coming to restore fellowship and His love with humanity. The carpenter was Jesus Christ. I learned that Jesus Christ was not Superman. In the temptation narratives (Matt. 4; Luke 4), Satan tempted him to indulge in selfish displays of divine power. Doing those things was very irrelevant to his mission and purpose. That is not to say that he was powerless. But his power was the power of pulling humanity out of its sin and enabling it to reject those things that plague or threaten human life. These passages of scripture examine the magnitude and purpose of his power. They inform us that he is not some superman that comes to the rescue us because he has heard of a crime being committed on some news bulletin. No, this passage shows Jesus as God, coming to empower and redeem a lost humanity. He is not a visitor from another planet doubling as a human being. He is God coming to live among His creatures to deliver them from the thrall of sin and evil. A closer look at His power then provides us with a better understanding of who He is and what His coming means for us who live today. This lesson examines two things: His power over external storms that beset and threaten humanity (vv. 35-41) and his power to calm evil's internal storms that rob human life of its vitality (5:1-13).

WHAT MANNER OF MAN IS THIS?
(MARK 4:35-41)

The point of this passage comes in verse 41, wherein the disciples ask the question, "Who is this?" It is a question later answered by the least expected (the demon-possessed man) as the disciples become increasingly aware that they are in the midst of one whose power is indescribable.

This passage continues the theme of Jesus' authority and power referred to in Mark 1:16-28; 2:1-12. Yet, like the religious leaders, the disciples continuously refuse to under-stand the width, breadth, and purpose of His power. Previously, Jesus has healed a multitude of people with detailed accounts of His exorcism of a demon-possessed man and the forgiveness of sin of a crippled man. His past established Him as a person of divine authority who does what only God can do (2:6-7). In this study, Jesus displays His power over nature in commanding a turbulent storm to subside, and then, He quells the inward but severe storm that is driving a fellow human mad. These passages empha-size Jesus' ability and willingness to confront those things that bring disaster into human life in an effort to reconcile humanity to God. This conflict with the storm and evil foreshadows His own conflict with death and presupposes His ability to handcuff it. Those confronted with isolation on the sea of life and those who live day to day within that realm of death, all find a safe refuge in Jesus. This passage shows the urgency and need for the power that Jesus brings with him. The disciples and the demon-possessed man are desperate. This desperation is a call for faith in Jesus' abili-ty to rid humanity of evil calamities. This need for faith is verified in the fearful disposition of the disciples and others who are terrified of Jesus after His broad display of divine authority and power.

The passage begins with Jesus suggesting that the group take a brief reprieve from their evangelistic activities by crossing over to the other side of the sea. On the way, Jesus takes a nap. After a hard day of preaching, the Lord suffers from physical exhaustion. Mark shows Jesus sleeping, a human act and a human need. Here is not someone mas-querading in human flesh but one who shares in the humanity of those He has come to save in God's love net. The scene of Jesus' sleeping begins a series of contrasts that ultimately lead to conflict. The disciples are fishermen by trade and are the experts or are at the very least experienced seamen. In contrast, Jesus was a carpenter and had limited experience as a mariner. Yet, when the storm rises and envelops the boat, the expert seamen are the ones rattled, while the carpenter remains asleep, unperturbed by the squalling sea.

The sea at storm with Jesus asleep at the stern, calls to mind the Old Testament story of Jonah who slumbers on a boat headed for Tarsus. In Jonah's case, the only way to quiet the storm was for the crew to toss the disobedient, itinerant preacher overboard (Jonah 1). The book reveals, however, that although the sea storm abates, a far deeper storm continues to brew in Jonah. Jonah is discontented with God over his saving of Nineveh. Jonah felt that the Assyrians had no right to receive God's forgiveness, especially since they committed acts of atrocity against God's chosen people. Jonah's account finds the prophet left wanting when compared to the Markian Jesus. In this passage, in contrast to Jonah, Jesus, the obedient preacher of God, awakens not to be tossed overboard or discussed as the subject of the crew's discontent, but to command the sea to be quiet and still. The sea hears and recognizes the voice of its creator and immediately obeys.

When Jesus speaks, He does what God does. In Genesis 1, God spoke and the earth and all of its fixtures came into being. At the word of God, things happen. In Mark 2, Jesus spoke words of forgiveness and the crippled man's paralysis left him. In the same passage, He commanded an evil spirit to come out of a man. Now, Jesus speaks commanding the storm to "shut up!" and it does. He does only what God can do. In commanding the wind and the sea to desist its ferocious activity, Jesus displays who He is and the elements of nature recognize him. The only non-recognizing entity is the normal people around Him that He created in His image.

The theme of sleeping here is not like Jonah's slumber, which is an attempt to ignore God, neither is it an account of unconcern as implied in the disciples' question to him. Nature is only acting out the course of its life. His sleep is a result of His physical exhaustion and fatigue from a strenuous evangelistic campaign on the shore.

The text is sure to note that in His sleep he is not awed by such force, for it is He who has supplied nature with it. He rises calmly to calm the raging sea. Notice the absence of panic in his demeanor and voice. Mark catches another contrast: He is calm, but they are hysterical and desperate. Thus, their desperation and fear results in their thoughtless question.

This question to Him about caring reflects also on His inexperience as a fisherman. Jesus is a carpenter by trade as opposed to them making their livelihood on the sea. It is ironic at first glance that the perceived experts of the sea call desperately for help upon one unskilled in water navigation, one who is a carpenter. They probably need him to man the oar in an effort to continue their strength, with the hopes of surviving this terrible sea storm.

Yet, their turning to Jesus, the carpenter by trade, is the only recourse they have, and in some seminal way, they recognize that. Jesus rises, speaks a word, and the tension is over. The disciples ask, "Who is this?" His act of authority provokes a sense of fear that, in their midst, is someone of unspeakable power.

It is important to remember the disciples' question, "Who is this?" For their inquest, though it reveals their fear, calls for us to trust in Jesus at all times and in all situations. It should not be expected that our association with Him means the elimination of all life's storms. No! Storms are a part of what it means to live freely. It does mean that when storms occur, and occur they will, they must trust who Jesus is and in His care for them.

POWER TO QUELL INTERNAL STORMS (MARK 5:2-13)

This passage re-emphasizes whom Jesus is by focusing on His power to quell internal storms in humanity caused by demonic inhabitation. It is a display of His great, divine ability over nature and the sea. Taken together, the two pericopes are a vivid testimony of his power over both land and sea. It is an elaboration of Genesis I. In that passage, God spoke and brought land and water out of chaos. Here, Jesus does the same thing.

Once again, the issue of death emerges. The disciples are confronted with their own demise as they desperately seek Jesus' help. Now when they have crossed over, He is confronted by a man who lives among the tombs, who lives among the dead in the realm of death.

This man possessed extraordinary strength, but not enough to reject the inner turmoil he is experiencing in his own life. He cannot be bound, as shown by the narrator's observation of the breaking of chains. However, he is indeed helpless to help himself. The evil spirit in him has full control of him. It is also ironic that the sequence of events that took place in earlier chapters is related to this story in that the demon-possessed man readily answers the question of who Jesus is.

Two things are important here: even the ungodly recognize who Jesus is and confess to His power, a power and presence that troubles the disciple and religious leader alike. On the other hand, the evil spirit's reaction to Jesus contrasts that of the religious leaders in chapter 2.

The movement of Jesus to the other side is a scene shift. This shift suggests that Satan has laid his claim on this area and implies that Jesus' encounter with the evil spirit will not be a pleasant or easy one. Satan will not easily let go of those areas he has held in his evil scheme of things for so long. As it stands, this man is subjected to inner storms of satanic forces as the disciples at sea are ravaged by torrential winds and walloping waves. Chaotic forces beyond their control propel both. Both, desperately, come to Jesus, and both receive relief beyond belief.

As stated, the man with the evil spirit lives among the dead and has living inside him the one whose objective is his death and the total destruction of humanity. Thus, Jesus encounters those things that seek to rob humanity of its life and vitality.

This man's life is wrecked. What happened to him could have easily happened to the disciples on the sea, had not Jesus intervened. But the probability of wreckage is not an option for this man. It is a fact of life. His mode of dress speaks loudly for the state of affairs in which his life is parked. His life is a wreck. He lived in apparent isolation from God and the community, and the community's answer to his sad life was to bind him and isolate him. They protected themselves. One human life on the fringe of destruction living among the dead was of no apparent concern to them. He could not be domesticated or tamed. That is to say, he could not be forced to exhibit any resemblance or behavior that allowed them to remotely consider rehabilitating him (how often and how quick is society to lock away and incarcerate rather than rehabilitate those considered to be, as well as guilty of, social mishaps).

The word tame here underscores society's negative reaction and revulsion to this troubled life. His behavior is not human; it is animalistic and wild. Therefore, people treat him according to his actions. Thrust out of mainline society, he is forced to live with those who will not be disturbed by his exaggerated and ungodly behavior. His life is a scene of death in the midst of death. Both he and society, which has isolated him, are powerless to overcome his state of chaos and his state of death.

The man confronts Jesus with statements of recognition, and a plea. Jesus gets to the root of the problem. The man's problem is not his exaggerated behavior. The behavior is only a symptom of a deeper problem living within him. The man's problems are an abundance of evil spirits living within him. Earlier we witnessed Jesus' ability to thoroughly diagnose the human situation when He offered forgiveness of sin to the paralyzed man (chapter 2).

In ordering the evil spirit out of the man, Jesus shows the pervasiveness of evil. Evil desires to live and to live in such a way as to thrive and prosper. However, the prosperity is built upon a platform of utter selfishness. It wants to live. Yet, its life is always parasitic. Notice how the evil spirit pleads with Jesus for mercy to let it live. But it had no mercy on this poor miserable soul. Moreover, it uses a delay tactic to stall its apparent exorcism. It pleads with Jesus to allow it to find a new residence. The slick and slimy character of evil is elusive like a snake. It sneaks and hides behind every rock and crevice. First, it questions Jesus even though it knows it is completely answerable to the "Holy One" of God. Second, it seeks to manipulate Jesus by calling His name. The evil spirit's display of the messianic secret is not the desire to worship Him, but because it wants to put Him on the defensive. By recognizing Him in the public arena, the Spirit makes it more difficult for the religious leaders and others to accept Jesus for who He is. These leaders have already wrongly concluded that Jesus' power comes from Satan. Being identified by the evil spirit probably affirms this in the minds of the skeptics. The demon's purpose is to bring calamity upon humanity and to undermine the ministry of Jesus. But in its evasiveness, it is the one who is destroyed. The legions of evil spirits enter the swine and the swine's violent reaction of running into the sea destroyed both the swine and the evil group of spirits. This passage points to the self-destructiveness of evil. Its attempt to live by evading exorcism leads to its own demise. Jesus sets the man free and allows the spirits of evil to fall into its own pit of destruction. It is indicative of the storms we face in life. This passage shows how the power of God is not limited to calming the storms of nature but can conquer all types of storms that beset humanity.

SUMMARY

Jesus has authority over all life. Those things that affect us by way of the environment, outside conditions, and even the thoughtless deeds of others must submit to the power of Jesus. Those things that cause internal anxiety are also responsible to the ability of Christ. We have access to this great power by submitting ourselves to His care.

These pericopes of scripture are important for contemporary humanity. They show that Jesus' power is equivalent to the task of saving humanity from external and internal forces that seek to destroy it. However, the stories call for faith in Jesus' ability and presence with us. Even though the story projects Jesus sleeping, it assures us that His sleep is never to our detriment. We are called to trust and to have faith. To do so, we must know who He is. He is none other than the "Holy One" of God. He is the One who created both land and sea and all therein. Thus, all forces of life are under His sovereignty. The incident of the evil spirit reinforces this point. The demons recognized Him and knew that exorcism by simple utterance of a word would judge their fate. In Jesus, evil will not be allowed to continuously wreak havoc into human life. The community may isolate, incarcerate its social misfits, but Jesus gets to the root of their problems, restores them as full persons. Knowing who He is, then, becomes our basis for trust and faith.

DISCUSSION QUESTIONS

1. Why did Jesus come to the world?

2. Why did the Jewish people fail to recognize Jesus?

3. What are the consequences for the failure to recognize Him?

4. How can we come to know Him better and to experience His power?

5. When we speak of God's love for us in Jesus, what are some concrete ways this love for us is evident?

Section II

LIVE BY THE SPIRIT

CHAPTER FIVE

Faith and Works
— Galatians: 1:1-2, 6-9; 2:15-21 —
"The Only Way to Go"

We have come to believe in Christ Jesus, so that we might be justified by faith in Christ, and not by doing the works of the law (Gal. 2:16, NRSV).

INTRODUCTION

Can Christians work and earn their salvation by keeping the Ten Commandments and other laws like them, or can they do whatever they want and then run to the church, pray to God in Jesus Christ and make everything alright? These passages of scripture resolve any confusion Christians may have in understanding the source of their salvation and what they are to do in light of it. Its primary purpose is to provide the explanation of complex theological technical terms like "justification by faith," "righteousness," and "works." Paul desires to show that reconciliation to God comes through the power and gift of God. It is not the product of human initiative, human achievement, or human ability. Rather it is our faith in the perfect life of Jesus Christ that sets us right before God. Paul seeks to lead us to this truth by recounting his authority as an apostle (vv. 1-2), by providing the occasion for this letter (vv. 6-9), and giving the facts of the one true gospel (2:15-21).

PAUL'S AUTHORITY AS AN APOSTLE
(GALATIANS 1:1-2)

The book of Galatians opens with Paul identifying himself as an apostle sent by Jesus Christ and God the Father. His claim to have derived his apostolic authority from God provides the foundation upon which Paul establishes his argument that Christians are justified by faith in Jesus Christ. Paul's claim to have been sent by Jesus and God the Father supercedes any Jewish reference or claim to the Law of Moses as the basis for salvation. In using the term "apostle" and providing it as the source of his authority, Paul is establishing himself as an official representative of God in Jesus Christ. Paul saw himself as an apostle, parallel to and on equal footing with the "Twelve," even if he was "last of all" (1 Cor. 5:7-8; Gal. 1:17-19; Rom. 1:1). Thus he writes as one who has been personally called by Christ. He saw the role of the apostles to be a special one in Christian history and was convinced that they performed a crucial function in the establishment of the faith in the period just after the Resurrection. Therefore, Paul expects the Galatians to listen. He writes to them with the authority of the Lord Jesus Christ, and they are to accept his teachings without dissension or dialogue.

OCCASION FOR THE LETTER
(GALATIANS 1:6-9)

These verses explain Paul's reason for writing this letter. The Christians at Galatia have changed positions in relationship to the Gospel they had received from Paul. Paul expresses his amazement that they would be so easily misled or diverted from the truth. His concern is that they were persuaded by others to follow a perverted gospel that was indeed no gospel at all. In the congregation were Jewish Christians called "Judaizers" who did not fully accept Paul's preaching of believers being justified or set right with God by faith in the death, burial, and resurrection of Jesus Christ. These people did not believe that faith in Jesus Christ could replace or supercede the Law of Moses as the way to please God. They felt that the two existed in a kind of mutual relationship. The apostle immediately saw this distortion of the true message of

God and of what God had done in Jesus Christ. Paul moved immediately to correct this false doctrine or "heresy."

The terms in verse 8 "we preached to you" and "than what you accepted" refers to the same true gospel of God's redemption in Jesus. It is Paul's way of telling them that only the message they received originally from him was true because it had been given to him by direct revelation from God himself and given to them just as he had received it. Therefore, not even Paul had the authority to change or present to them a different gospel. The Good News they received derived not from Paul, but from Jesus Christ Himself. Paul says that anyone who preaches or accepts a different message is therefore accursed. Paul invokes the wrath of God on all those people who distort the Gospel of God's gracious gift of justification by faith in Jesus Christ and substitute the Law of Moses for it. Notice the breadth of Paul's apostolic authority. His authority allowed him to provide the basis for Christian faith to the Galatians on the one hand and to criticize them and others who sought to minimize the central role of Jesus in the Christian faith on the other. This letter, then, is written to deal with the development of a false gospel that minimizes what God did in Jesus Christ to reconcile the world unto himself.

THE ONE TRUE GOSPEL
(GALATIANS 2:15-21)

These verses drive home Paul's earlier teachings to the Galatians. They are a detailed explanation of complex terms such as "justification by faith" and "works of the law." In this section that I have entitled the "one true Gospel," the meaning of each of these terms will be fleshed out in hopes of providing to Christians a greater understanding of Christianity. In verses 15 and 16 Paul demonstrates the common conversion experience he shared with Peter and with other Jewish Christians. They were Jews by birth. To be a Jew by birth was indeed a blessed privilege because Israel had been given God's covenant and promises (Rom. 3:1-2; 9:4-5). This perceived privilege led to Jews labeling non-Jewish people or Gentiles as "sinners" because they did not have the law and obey it, nor did they have the customary laws regulating diet, days of worship, worship activities, tithing, circumcision, and other matters. The law—having it and observing it—separated Jews from Gentiles. Furthermore, Gentiles were deemed sinful because they were uncircumcised, ate unclean food, and fellowshipped with unclean people.

But in verse 16, Paul, a privileged Jew, recounts his and Peter's conversion experience. They both came to the conviction that human beings are not justified by observing the law, but by faith in Jesus Christ. Thus justification by faith is an important theological concept central to the life of the Christian faith. Justification is a word that expresses our acceptance by God. It is based on the following scenario. Humanity finds itself guilty before God because it transgressed God's law and commandments. Humanity's desire and only hope is that God will somehow forgive it, restore it to his fellowship, and eliminate its guilt. But since God cannot simply overlook sin, humanity finds itself in a tough fix. But miraculously, God forgives; his forgiveness comes through Jesus Christ who assumes human guilt and bore the curse of the law in His death on the cross. Therefore, because of God's gracious activity in Jesus Christ, those who trust in Christ and give themselves to Him are restored to His fellowship. Sinful humanity has a new status and is accepted by God the righteous judge because of this process of justification. God then grants His Spirit so that human beings are continually transformed to live a life that exemplifies the character of Christ. So for Paul and Peter, humanity is not justified by observing the law.

"Works of the Law," as it is meant here, is the belief that ultimate acceptance by God comes only through a commitment to the "Law of Moses." It is trust in the exhibition of one's behavior that distinguishes Jews from Gentiles. The Jewish people believed if they kept the law as written they were saved. Thus by their exclusive holding of the law they were practically the only ones saved and the only ones striving toward righteousness. Therefore, the Law of Moses, according to the Judaizers, was as important as Jesus Christ, if not more so. It was this equivocation of the law with justification by faith in Jesus that disturbed Paul. Paul's argument is that the activity of God in Jesus Christ goes beyond the law. The two cannot stand together side-by-side. They are not equal. The common Jew felt that not conforming to the law was to live a lawless and sinful life. Leaving the law or submitting to it under Christ meant abandoning God's moral will.

But Paul explains in Gal. 2:17-21 that turning to Jesus by expressing faith in him and what he had done was the only true way to acknowledge a person's sinfulness. Turning to Christ was a turn to righteousness. The righteousness of Christ was imputed (put in) by faith. Christians then live a life in the power of the Spirit, which works in them to bring about a change in their thoughts, words, and deeds.

Consequently, what was found only in the law for the Jews, God has made available to all people. So the law, though useful for a season, has become obsolete. One is justified only by faith in Jesus Christ. So Paul contends that by believing in Jesus, one is crucified with Him to the law, and the resurrection of Christ grants new life to the believer. This means that believers are victorious and live a life that is no longer condemned by the law because of human failure to meet its requirements. Rather, because the believer is now indwelt by Christ, the power of the Holy Spirit now guides and controls the life of the believer.

As a result of leaving the law and accepting Jesus Christ, one is not setting aside God's grace or living a lawless, sinful life. Paul argues that the ones setting aside and missing out on God's grace are those who do not accept Jesus Christ alone as the way to God. If a proper standing before God could have been achieved by obeying the law, then there would not have been any need for Christ. But the irony is that these Judaizers have already confessed that Christ was God's agent for salvation. It is this confession that Paul urges the Galatian Christians to return to.

SUMMARY

This lesson is a complicated one because it presents the central core of the Christian faith. We need to understand these important points. Christians are saved by faith in the death, burial, and resurrection of Jesus Christ, alone. A mark of our faith and salvation is that Christians seek to obey the word of God and live out their lives as a testimony to him. This testimony is a life of service to God by serving others in love. The good deeds committed by a Christian do not save him or her before God. Our righteousness cannot present us faultless. Since we are human, we sin in one way or another. Our faith in Jesus Christ cleanses us, and God grants us His Spirit to help us rise above our imperfections. Therefore Christians must constantly seek God's Spirit as they strive to become more like Jesus Christ, our great example of love and righteousness.

Being caught in the love net compels us to live a corresponding lifestyle. the good news is, we are not alone. Jesus lives in us and walks with us to secure us as those who live by the power of His Spirit.

DISCUSSION QUESTIONS

1. Who were the Judaizers?

2. What were they trying to do?

3. Why did Paul write this book to the Galatians?

4. What are some of the lessons you have learned from this study? What is the relevance of being caught in the love net for this study?

5. Why is this book significant for Christians who live now?

6. What are some of the issues people face that vie for their allegiance and devotion to Christ?

CHAPTER SIX
Live the Gospel

— Romans 12:1-3, 9-21 —
"What is It All About"

Do not be conformed to this world, but be transformed by the renewing of your minds, so that you may discern what is the will of God—what is good and acceptable and perfect (Rom. 12:2).

INTRODUCTION

Our lesson calls upon believers to be different from their earthly peers and neighbors. It calls upon them to change their lives by undergoing a mind transformation. It calls upon one to change his or her behavior by changing the way one thinks. But the question arises, how can this be done? Paul has just admonished the Jewish people for persisting in their determination to pursue their own course of self-righteousness as the way to please God. Is Paul now contradicting himself? Of course not! Paul is appealing to Christians at Rome to allow God to change them through the power of the Holy Spirit. This inward change of mind is to be reflected in their outward lifestyle. His appeal is to contemporary Christians also. God wants us to change toward Him and unto life everlasting.

CHRISTIANS ARE TO BE A TRANSFORMED PEOPLE (ROMANS 12:1-2)

In Phil. 2:5 Paul urges Christians to adopt the mind of Christ, who dedicated his life to doing the will of God. In this passage from Rom. 12, Paul is calling upon believers to make the same radical decision to invest their lives by seeking to do the will of God. He calls upon believers to give their lives as a sacrifice to God. This type of sacrifice has two features. First, Paul calls upon them to be non-conformists or not unduly influenced by the society or community in which they live, and second, to allow God to change them through His power. Through implication, Paul is referring to the power of God in the Holy Spirit, which empowered believers in massive numbers after Jesus' resurrection from the dead. Paul is actually referring to what Christian doctrine calls "sanctification." Sanctification is the process of allowing God to clean and renew us daily so that we may be set apart to fully serve him. This chapter focuses on the practical aspects of the Christian life. To be a Christian is to practice living out the new life that Paul has already thoroughly explained in Romans chapters 1-11. The will of God is for Christians and others not only to know how and why they are justified by faith in Jesus, but also to show that the righteousness of Christ resides in them.

THE NEED FOR SELF-EVALUATION (ROMANS 12:3)

Paul has just recently admonished the Jewish people for their continued indulgence in self-righteousness. They failed to accept God's gift of Jesus as the way of salvation. Instead of accepting God's gift, they became so engrossed in self-righteousness that they looked down upon others who they thought were not as righteous as they. Thus they elevated themselves above the very people they were chosen to lead to God. In their arrogance they failed to be the beacon of light that God called them to be. In verse 3, Paul cautioned Christians at the Roman church to be mindful of how they viewed others. He cautioned them lest they practiced the same arrogance as their Jewish counterparts and became entangled in their own perceived "righteousness." Paul reminded them that their faith and obedience and gifts were not of their own making, but they were gifts from God. Therefore, they had no basis for elevating themselves and denigrating others. Simply put, they were not to be condescending to others. Their faith was a gift from God and designed to be used in the service of God. Thus a proper evaluation of themselves served to remind them that the righteousness they possessed was not their own. It is the righteousness of Jesus Christ imputed in them by the power of God through the Holy Spirit. Being caught in the love net of God is to see ourselves in a different light; we are a part of a team that works together for the advancement of the kingdom of God.

Love Is the Main Characteristic of Christian Living (Romans 12:9-21)

Verses 9-21 carry the theme of love as the main characteristic of Christian living. Christian life is to be characterized and identified by the badge of love. This badge is not a metal pendant or cross to be worn on one's outward apparel as a jewelry accessory or fashion statement. It is the presence of God Himself in the life of the Christian. Paul points out three things about love in relationship to Christian living: Love and the reaction to it (v. 9); the meaning of love (vv. 10-13 and 15-16); and love as it affects the attitude of Christians toward others (vv. 14, 17-21).

The ninth verse illustrates love as the secret of Christian conduct. It is the underlying principle, which creates, maintains, and characterizes the church. Love underlines the whole of God's redemptive activity in Jesus Christ. In Gal. 2:20, Paul explained "The life which I now live in the flesh I live by the faith of the Son of God, who loved me, and gave himself for me" (NRSV). In short, we love Him because He first loved us. Love characterizes the sacrificial life of Jesus Christ, and as His followers, it must also characterize the lives of all Christians, especially the lives of Christian leaders and workers. Our love for others must reflect or mirror His love for us. Therefore, it must be real, serious, and discriminating. It should help us to see more clearly the redemptive purposes of God and the need of others for God. Once we see clearly God's purpose, it leads us to action, to reach out and embrace others. This love then compels us to live out the mandates of the golden rule by treating others the way we desire to be treated by them.

Paul also demonstrates the character of love as it should be practiced in the Christian community. Love manifests itself in kindness and warm affection. Christians are a community. Thus their love must exemplify the concept of familial relationships. They are also to follow the imperative to rejoice in the new hope that has been given to them in Jesus Christ. They are to exhibit their faith and trust in the power of God in the midst of crisis and other trouble, and staunchly depend on God through the vehicle of prayer (vv. 10-13 and 15-16).

Finally, Paul urges them to share the community spirit by pooling their spiritual resources in an attempt to aid one another. Christians are not a group of isolated individuals that meet on Sunday by accident, but they are a community of believers who support, love, nurture and care for one another. The concept of the love net is the idea that we are one in the Lord God and are responsible for one another's welfare.

SUMMARY

The point of this lesson is that Christians must practice the Gospel. Often we believe that living out the Gospel is only for pastors and other church leaders. Not so! God calls us to the transformed life regardless of our age, occupation, social standing, etc. None are exempt from living according to the mandates of the Gospel. Although they face certain criticism for being different, different they must be. It is criticism they should welcome because they have the presence and power of God in their lives. God calls adults, youths, and children to be transformed. This transformation is shown in their daily walk.

We need to know that living a life that glorifies God is not easy. We will face tremendous pressure and rejection for holding to our faith. Yet it is a faith worth holding on to. Not only will we reap the benefit of living a more purposeful and blessed life, but we will spare ourselves many of the problems and heartaches that those who live without God, outside of His love net, have.

DISCUSSION QUESTIONS

1. What does Paul mean when he encourages Christians to "be transformed"?

2. Why is love the main characteristic of Christians?

3. How does the gift of God's Son affect our relationship with each other?

4. Rather than using violence as a weapon, how does the Christian fight evil? Provide three ways to do this.

5. Compare and contrast the concept of God's love net with human pride and human selfishness.

CHAPTER SEVEN

Live by the Spirit

— Galatians 5:16—6:5, 7-9 —

"Which Way do You Choose?"

Live by the Spirit, I say, and do not gratify the desires of the flesh (Gal. 5:16).

INTRODUCTION

Paul called upon his readers to acknowledge the freedom they had gained through their faith in Jesus Christ. In this passage he clarifies what he means by a "life of freedom." Freedom is living in the Spirit. This clarification comes in response to the Judaizers' claim that without the Law of Moses as a guide, the Galatians would suffer a relapse and fall back into a pagan lifestyle. "Not so," Paul replies. They are to walk or live in the Spirit (Gal. 5:16—5:26). He then illustrates to them the results of the spiritual life (Gal. 6:1-5, 7-9).

LIVE IN THE SPIRIT
(GALATIANS 5:16—5:26)

In seeking to clarify what he means by a life of freedom, Paul urges his readers to live in the Spirit. Paul sets up an interesting argument here. He responds to the Judaizers' claim that without the Law of Moses to guide them the Galatian Christians would adopt a loose lifestyle and live reckless sinful lives. Paul's response is to elaborate on what living in the Spirit means.

Life in the Spirit prohibits indulging in the flesh. In Gal. 5:15, Paul emphasizes that the Galatians are to serve one another in love. It is evident from his stress on "serving one another in love" that the church at Galatia is undergoing some internal strife. The false doctrine taught by the Judaizers led to internal dissension and to what Paul believes to be unChristian behavior. Therefore, he goes a step further to explain to his readers how they should act. Those who live in the Spirit are not to let their flesh control them, but they are to allow the Spirit to do so. They are in a war. It is a war between the Spirit and the flesh. It is a battle over God's will. Those who are engaged in this battle recognize that flesh and spirit are opposites. They are opposed to one another in much the same way that law is opposed to grace. When one lives in the Spirit one does not do what God's Spirit frowns upon. Living in the Spirit is a life of consistent surrender to God. Paul then provides further clarification. The "works of the flesh" can be divided into three categories: sex, worship, and social relationships.

There is nothing wrong with the sex drive itself; it is the gift of God. When it is under the influence of the Spirit, sex expresses the beauty of God's love for us and the love of a married couple for each other. It leads to the building of a home and a life of intimacy and sharing in which each marital partner thrives, finds fulfillment, enjoyment, and appreciation. But when it is under the influence of the flesh, sex results in immorality, impurity, and licentiousness. It leads to pre-marital and extra-marital intercourse that has little or no regard for the persons' total well being. Sex overshadows the whole of the human relationship, leading to promiscuous sexual activity, devoid of any sense of decency and shame. The world in which Paul preached was riddled with sexual dissolution, both natural and perverted. Here he stresses that such activities are "works of the flesh" and are not to be a part of the Christian lifestyle (v. 19).

In verse 20, Paul speaks of the sin of bad worship and of broken social relationships. This thinking seems to indicate that an improper understanding of worship and the place of God in human life, automatically lead to fragmentation in human relationships. Under the influence of the Spirit, human beings fulfill their need and purpose to know and worship God. This leads to deliverance from sin and from its power of destruction through faith in Jesus Christ. But when this need for worship comes under the domination of the flesh, it leads to idolatry, the tragic event where people worship the gods of their own creation, and to the elevation of technology to the status of God.

This verse also deals with social relationships. Under the influence and control of the Spirit, humanity develops meaningful and wholesome relationships, establishes good community life, and shares skills and resources that maximize human enjoyment and prosperity. But when dominated by the flesh, enmity, strife, jealousy, anger, selfishness, dissension, party spirit, envy, drunkenness, carousing, and a host of evil companions abound. Paul warns that those who participate in such activities are not living in the Spirit, but in the flesh, and as a result they forfeit their inheritance in the kingdom of God.

In verses 22-23a, Paul describes the life that lives in the Spirit. These verses are commonly called the "Fruits of the Spirit." Love is the essential quality of a spirit-filled life. This fruit includes all that the law requires of us in our relationship to others. We are to love others as Christ who gave himself on the cross loved us. The next fruit is joy because the Christian is firmly anchored in God's grace so that not even the most adverse circumstances can overcome us. Peace accompanies joy because it shows our confidence in God's love and ability to take care of us. The Spirit also works to make us even-tempered so that we act thoughtfully, patiently and kindly. The Spirit also produces the fruits of generosity, fidelity, and self-control. Self-control describes an inner strength depicting the presence of God himself in the human life.

Paul goes on to say that society needs no protection from those who bear these qualities. In Christ Jesus, they have crucified the flesh with its passions and desires. Therefore, he urges Christians to walk in the Spirit. By walking in the Spirit, he means a continuous striving to do God's will.

THE RESULT OF LIVING IN THE SPIRIT
(GALATIANS 6:1-5, 7-9)

Paul concludes this section with a set of imperatives directing Christians on how to treat one another. These imperatives or commands are elaborations of the Christian's walk in the Spirit. They are specific actions that must be done. Christians are to restore those who are overtaken in their trespasses. Mature Christians who possess the special fruit of "gentleness" and who are constantly evaluating themselves are the ones to be entrusted with this delicate ministry. They must work also to hold one another accountable to live as followers of Jesus. They must exercise care in the way they discipline those members of the family who go astray. Both the community and the one who errs are to reflect the character of the Lord. As those who live in the Spirit, they must act to mend the community to bring about peace. Christians are to correct one another, but it must be done in the spirit of gentleness. As others are reproved, Paul calls upon them to evaluate themselves by the Spirit so as to avoid the temptation to judge and evaluate the erring person too harshly. Paul seems to be reminding the Galatians that they too were once in need of grace and forgiveness (and might be again). So the proper attitude one should have in restoring one who has erred is that which compares his righteousness to the righteousness of Christ (vv. 1-5, 7-9).

SUMMARY

This lesson shows Christians how to live in the Spirit of God. It points out the differences between "life in the flesh" and "life in the Spirit." To live in the Spirit Christians must avoid pre-marital and extra-marital sex and reject the world's presentation of any type of sex outside of the marital union as okay. They are to hold to the worship of God and refuse to make automobiles, good looks, celebrities, lewd dances, sports, and other things their God. They must avoid human strife and conflict. They must not see others as beneath them. They are to show they possess the Spirit of God by living a life of love, helping others to see God in them.

DISCUSSION QUESTIONS

1. What does Paul mean by the term "live in the flesh"?

2. What are the characteristics of those who live in the flesh?

3. What does Paul mean by the term "live in the Spirit"?

4. What are the characteristics of those who live in the Spirit?

5. What is the end result of living in the Spirit?

6. How does living in the Spirit compare with living in the love net?

CHAPTER EIGHT

Call to Freedom

— Galatians 5:15 —

"We've Been Set Free"

You were called to freedom, brothers and sisters; only do not use your freedom as an opportunity for self-indulgence, but through love become slaves to one another (Gal. 5:13, NRSV).

INTRODUCTION

This topic of discussion has two points, "the perils of legalism" (vv. 1-12) and "the perils of libertinism" (vv. 13-15). Paul saw the Galatians as those who had to make some hard choices. They could listen to and be persuaded by Judaizers to revert to a strict observance of the law, they could lapse back into their former life of heathenism, or they could hold fast to the truth that Paul had preached to them in Christ Jesus. They had a choice to stay in the love net or to allow others to persuade them to get out of it. The choice was theirs to make.

THE PERILS OF LEGALISM
(GALATIANS 5:1-2)

Paul opens up this passage by making an important announcement to the Galatians,—they had been set free in Christ Jesus. He urges them to keep their freedom and refuse to be forced into slavery again. But what are they freed from or subject to become slaves to? In the second verse Paul uses the emphatic pronoun and his name for impact. The use of both of these refer to his authority as an apostle so that the Galatians are to weigh carefully whatever is being taught in the congregation by the Judaizers over against what Paul says about the situation.

The peril of legalism is this: if they succumb to the insistence of the Judaizers that they submit to circumcision, they give up all the freedom they had been given in Jesus Christ. In fact, by doing so they are placing themselves in a position where they will have to obey every iota of the law. They cannot be selective here; the law is not a cafeteria line where some items may be chosen and others ignored. Verse 4 points out this contrast as well. Accept the law and circumcision and you will effectively separate yourself from Christ (and all the freedom he offers). Accept the law as necessary to a right standing with God and find yourself alienated from God because the law nullifies grace (see Rom. 7:2-6). The two, circumcision and Christ, the law and grace, are not mutually exclusive. To turn to the law is to lose totally one's position and status in Christ. That is to say, there is no hope in being justified before God by the law. Rather the hope of the Galatians is the hope based upon a faith commitment in Jesus Christ. It is hope that came in the receiving of God's Spirit given through the preaching of the Gospel of God's grace in Jesus Christ and works to transform believers to the will of God. This hope is fulfilled in the "day of judgment." Paul makes the great announcement that neither the law nor any other religious teachings matter. All that matters is faith in Jesus Christ. This faith is the trusting response to God's grace in the death, burial, and resurrection of Jesus Christ.

But this faith must not be a mere statement or verbal expression of one's tepid belief. It must be operative through love. Faith is fully a response of trust in God's initiative exhibited through a life of service to God by loving others.

At one time the Galatians were doing well, but something happened to throw them off stride. Paul assures them that it was not of God. He warns them this message that makes Christ secondary to the law does not have God as its source. The lies told by the Judaizers, who are a small group, is an evil influence that threatens them and the whole Christian community. Paul expresses high hopes as their father and apostle in the faith that they would adhere to the Gospel they heard from him.

Paul ends this section by warning the Galatians that false teachers would come under the judgment of God. Their doctrine of the law of circumcision, which they also falsely attributed to Paul, is a denial of the cross. Paul's anger is kindled by their lies. He would contradict himself by preaching the merits of circumcision. He replies by way of a cruel joke: "If they are so eager to start cutting on the male sex organ, I wish they would castrate themselves" (vv. 13-14). Thus, they would be cut off or severed not only from grace but from their own people. (See Deut. 23:1) To preach circumcision would be to negate the world-transforming power of the Gospel that had been divinely revealed to him. It would be the equivalent of returning to slavery.

PERILS OF LIBERTY
(GALATIANS 5:13-15)

The Galatians could not help but see the perils of legalism that Paul had placed before them. But there was another danger that he must also warn them of. Christian freedom released them from the legal requirement in seeking a right standing before God, and for some this meant that absence of legal requirements meant they could sit loosely and live haphazard lives. Paul warns them here that Christian freedom from the law is not a license to do "whatever" they please. He encouraged them to serve one another in love. Paul stressed practicing the "golden rule." The "It's my 'thang' and I can do what I want to do" attitude leads to condemnation by God and to the very destruction of our souls. The "It's my prerogative" disposition defies the Sovereignty of God and leaves us in direct opposition to His will. Those who insist that their lives are their own do not live in the freedom of God but have already subjected themselves to the slavery of sin. They have effectively severed their lives from God and from enclosure in the divine love net.

SUMMARY

God saves us through faith in Jesus Christ. This frees us from the legal requirements of the Law of Moses, but this freedom is not a license to live recklessly. Our freedom points to our ability to keep the law fully, so it in effect continually condemned us. The freedom also points to the grace of God, who provided to us the great example of love and righteousness in Jesus Christ and the power of the Holy Spirit to express our faith in a life of obedience to His will. This means our character must be one of love where we serve others and treat them as we desire to be treated.

DISCUSSION QUESTIONS

1. What does freedom mean?

2. What is the effect of making the law equivalent to Christ?

3. Why did Paul stop preaching circumcision?

4. Why does Paul call upon them to serve one another?

5. Why is the characteristic of love of vital importance for the Christian?

CHAPTER NINE

God's Glory Revealed

— Romans 8:18-27, 31-34, 38-39 —
"Does Anybody Care?"

I consider that the sufferings of this present time are not worth comparing with the glory about to be revealed to us. (Rom. 8:18, NRSV)

INTRODUCTION

Romans 8 is an important chapter because it focuses our attention on what it means to live in the "Spirit of God." This passage expresses how one is cleansed and set apart to live the life of God after one has been set right with God through the redemptive work of Jesus Christ. Therefore this unit of Scripture is one of encouragement to those who have committed their life to God in Jesus Christ. Believers are to take notice of three important things that serve to guide them in their Christian life, anticipation of their glorification (vv. 18-27), confirmation of divine protection and concern (vv. 31-34), and affirmation of God's loving presence with them (vv. 38-39). For those who are constantly barraged by and assaulted with new and immense troubles, Paul's pronouncement is especially important because it declares God's support for them as they desire to live for Him, and supplies His Spirit to help them do just that. That is to say, God provided not only a good example on how to live in sending His son, Jesus Christ, but He also supplied the power to live like Jesus in the giving of His Holy Spirit. In Jesus we are caught in God's love net of salvation and redemption.

SOMETHING TO LOOK FORWARD TO
(ROMANS 8:18-27)

The first parent's sin of disobedience introduced death and tragedy into the human family. Since they were the originators and progenitors of the human race, their sin darkened human existence and stained the whole of creation by corrupting it thoroughly. Humanity and all of creation stood in opposition to God. Unable to account or atone for its sin, humanity's salvation lay in the redemptive activity of God in Jesus Christ. Therefore, faith in the life, death, burial, and resurrection of Jesus, who lived a perfect life before God, justifies humanity and begins the process of cosmic redemption. Paul can then speak with bold assurance that Christians can anticipate the glorification of God in the new age. The old age encumbered with the doom and gloom that comes with sin cannot be compared to the new sinless age that is yet on the horizon. This new age is a reason for hope. It is hope that God is working to set things right in between then and now. God has given to us His Spirit as our guarantee that this new perfect sinless age will come to pass. The Spirit is God's stamp of approval that we have been adopted into His family and are set to inherit His bountiful blessings. So even though suffering is bad, it cannot compare with the glory that is on the way. What Christians are to do in the meantime is to live the victorious life that God provides through his Holy Spirit. Truly in Jesus' sacrifice God has given us something to look forward to.

SINCE HE DID IT, YOU CAN BELIEVE IT
(ROMANS 8:31-34)

Christians are reminded in this section that God guarantees a good outcome for them. After pointing out that God uses the circumstances of life, even the bad ones, for the ultimate "Good" of those who have expressed faith in him, Paul moves to reassure Christians of their permanent guarantee of God in the gift of His Son Jesus Christ. The question, "What shall we say to this?" in verse 31 is a question that is asked to stimulate the memory of God's enveloping gracious protection in three ways. God's care for us is shown in His gift of Jesus Christ as atonement from sin. This gift represents the extent of gracious protection. God did not withhold His Son Jesus and will not withhold any aspect of His love from us. He who has delivered you from sin and its penalty will protect you. He has overcome the greatest and final problem of death. Yes Jesus died. But God raised Him up from death. So that the one who came to set humanity right with God is also the one who continues to plead with God for us. His love then is astonishing: It delivers us from sin and sets us right before God, even when we fail. His love for us causes Him to represent us before God. He protects us. His protection is complete. We are hid with Christ in God. That is to say that we are caught in the love net of God's protection and glory. (Col. 3:14) Therefore, Paul can present an itemized list of things that are unable to come between God and us. The power of God's love and ability to keep those who defy the crowd and attempts of the devil to pull them away from Him is available to them. Does this mean that Christians will not be tempted, will not be redelivered, will not undergo peer pressure because of their commitment to live like Jesus. Of course not! But what it does mean is that whatever the situation, nothing can and will be able to come between them and God. Christ's love for them is the glue that keeps them connected.

CAUGHT IN THE LOVE NET
(ROMANS 8:38-39)

Paul loves to repeat himself. It is a reminder to "EACH OF US" that God's Word is trustworthy. In our country's earlier history many deals were made with only the word of the person and a handshake. Although it is good now days to have a legal contract to protect your interest against improprieties, we can be sure that God's Word is His bond. God never reneges on His promise. He has given us His Son to redeem us from sin and to set us right before Him. He provided the Holy Spirit to walk with us on a daily basis to sanctify us. Jesus Christ the only Son, who died and was raised from the dead by God intercedes for us also. Shall we fail? Shall He fail us in times of adversity? The response is a resounding No!!! We will "survive." We will make it through. We are caught in His net of love, protection, and grace. But the word "survivor" falls short and does not convey His combative ability to bring us through. We not only survive the ordeals of life, but we are "conquerors" over them. In Him we are victorious champions. Nothing in earth or heaven, or below them, nothing in the universe can overcome the God in whom we have placed our trust; therefore keep on living, and the victory which is already won will be yours.

SUMMARY

Life is not an exercise in futility. This passage of Scripture emphasizes God's involvement in human activity. Though terrible things take place in the world—bombings, rape, social injustice, murders, accidents, diseases, and other things—Paul attests that those who love God find a sense of protection, confidence that God cares for them. This care is manifest in the gift of God's only Son, Jesus Christ, on the cross. In and through Jesus, God overcame humanity's greatest and most persistent enemy—death. This means you can rest assured that God will continue to act in contemporary times for your benefit. You are caught in His love net of divine redemption.

DISCUSSION QUESTIONS

1. Why does Paul ask the question what then shall we say to these things?

2. How does Paul answer his own question?

3. What does this question and answer mean for Christians today?

4. What does the love of God in Christ Jesus mean for you?

5. How are you caught in God's love net?

Section III

CHRISTIAN

RIGHTEOUSNESS

CHAPTER TEN

The Way of the Righteous

— Psalms 1; 19:7-10 —

"The Right Way"

The Lord watches over the way of the righteous, but the way of the wicked will perish (Psalm 1:6, NRSV).

INTRODUCTION

Psalm 1 is an introduction to the whole book of Psalms. The word *psalm* means "song" or "hymn." These psalms are expressions that define life as it relates to God and others. There are different types of psalms: Praises to God; Royal Psalms; Laments; and minor types such as Wisdom and Reflective Psalms. Psalm 1 is of the latter category. It is a poem which gives expression to the entire book. It falls within the Old Testament pattern of Wisdom Literature, which provides instruction and guidance for living unto God. Psalm 19 is a psalm of praise in which the poet expresses the gloriousness of God's law. The combination of the two passages calls for reflection on the goodness of God who supplies His Word as our perfect guide to life. This lesson has three parts: it portrays the righteous (Psalm 1:1-3); it portrays the godless (vv. 4-6); and God's perfect law (19: 7-10).

PORTRAIT OF THE RIGHTEOUS (PSALM 1:1-3)

The word *blessed* here means "happy" just as it does in the Beatitudes. But the Old Testament pattern emphasizes that happiness must have an object or be internally possessed by an individual. So the term blessed is better translated in the instance as how rewarding it is for the person who conforms to a certain standard of living. This standard of living is expressed in both a negative and positive context.

The writer of this psalm seeks to illustrate the complete satisfaction one derives from not following the crowd and by putting one's trust in God. The crowd in this sense is composed of those who are ungodly. There is a triple pattern to show why one is blessed. The follower of God is not influenced by the ungodly and does not take or seek their advice or fellowship. The worshiper refuses to participate in activities and with people who flagrantly or casually dismiss God and defy His will for their lives. Such a person is destined for true happiness because the focus is on doing things God's way. The word law means in this context the teachings, instructions, and guidance of God. One finds fulfillment in the revelation of God. It is relevant, even essential to life, as the godly person constantly meditates upon it. Verse 3 further expounds in a figurative sense on what blessed means and the end result of delighting in the guidance of God. The comparative simile drives it home. Such a person is like a well-watered tree. This picture is especially important because Palestine suffered naturally from poor irrigation. The use of this figure of speech would get the attention of the poet's hearers and readers. The ever-flowing stream guarantees a good product or harvest. This tree is the epitome of good health. So is the person who delights in following God's guidance. Success is sure to follow them.

PORTRAIT OF THE UNGODLY
(PSALM 1:4-6)

The person dedicated to God's guidance prospers continually. But those who digress from doing God's will find just the opposite fate, the psalmist bluntly informs.

They do not prosper but are helpless before God as trash is before a strong wing. These verses re-emphasize the implication of verse 1. Verse 1 describes the blessed that refuse fellowship with the ungodly. By implication it describes the fate of those who do follow the advice, pattern of life, and fellowship of the wicked. They are like trash, worthless articles, which are scattered by the wind. The ungodly cannot remain in the place where justice and good are. Neither can they abide in the place where those who serve God congregate. Their way is directly opposed to God's will and God's way.

Furthermore God knows who they are, what they are doing, and has already judged them. However in great contrast to the previous verse, verse 6 points out God's intimate relationship with the righteous. Their future is bright and prosperous because they follow God's guidance. On the other hand, the future for those who delight in following or giving wicked advice, embark on a life of ungodliness, and fellowship with the unjust will not prosper. They are on the road to destruction. It is a case of the blind leading the blind.

GOD'S REVELATION OF THE LAW
(PSALM 19: 7-10)

Psalm 1:2-3 describes how the "righteous" make it their business to give themselves over to following God's will by depending upon His revelation of the law. Law as used here does not refer to the strict legalism of the Jews but to the guidance God provides through His teachings. The content of His teachings is provided in Psalm 19:7-10. He uses several terms that mean essentially the same thing to describe God's Word, law, testimony, commandments, fear, and ordinance. What is of major importance is what he says about them. In effect, he praises God's Word for its perfection because it is without flaw and refreshing to the soul. It is also sure, that is, it is dependable as its giver and educationally uplifting. It provides guidance to the naïve and inexperienced. The law of God is right, and as a result it produces an inner joy that comes from being in good standing or a right relationship with God. His imperatives are good and clean and perfect. They light up the path of life. The fear of the Lord, the reverence and worship of God, does not include any principle that corrupts or defiles. The ordinances of God are true. Thus God's guidance, as reflected in worship, and the keeping of it are the real treasure in the field that people should seek. It is the means to a prosperous and a dignified life. The result of such is a life completely fulfilled.

The point of these passages is that the one who is truly wise seeks God and revels in the law of God because it brings prosperity and fulfillment that those who do not seek God, follow His pattern for living, or seek His fellowship will never have. It is meaningful only to those who are embodied in God's divine love net.

SUMMARY

Two recommendations are made here. First, this study emphasizes that Christians make God's Word a source of constant reflection, and second, that they follow with great care the path that reflection upon God's Word suggests. Believers are encouraged to weigh carefully the advice and suggestions of their friends and others against the Word of God. They are encouraged to reflect upon God's Word before giving in to peer pressure and doing other things that stand as conditions of their being accepted by the crowd. The question we must ask ourselves is not what would Jesus do, but what would Jesus have me do?

DISCUSSION QUESTIONS

1. What do the terms "blessed" and "law" mean in Psalm 1?

2. What two types of people does the lesson describe?

3. What does it mean to find delight in the law of God?

4. What is the relationship between Psalm 1 and Psalm 19:7-10?

5. Why are the blessed caught in the love net?

CHAPTER ELEVEN

God of Justice

— Psalms 82; 113:5-9 —
"God is Judge"

Rise up, O God, judge the earth; for all the nations belong to you! (Psalm 82:8, NRSV)

INTRODUCTION

These two psalms attest to the fact that God is a God of Justice. Each of the psalms demonstrates that God is actively engaged in the course of human events and has set standards by which human beings should live in relationship with one another. When partiality is practiced by any of the creatures God has made (whether superhuman or human), it gets His attention and instant rebuke. Psalm 82 is a didactic psalm that was sung in the temple by the Levites. Its setting is the convening of the "heavenly council" where God addresses the council, its unjust actions among humanity. It ends with a call upon God to exercise His righteous judgment upon the earth. The difficulty some scholars have in interpreting this psalm is whether or not the word "god" in verses 1 and 6 refers to a group of lesser gods, angels, or human judges. A thorough examination of the context could include all three groups. The point of the psalm is that God will not tolerate injustice at any level by anyone. He is equally dismayed when barriers are erected that depict one group of human beings superior over another group and have this interpretation as a result of His will and blessings.

The 113th Psalm continues this theme of God as the God of Justice in verses 5-9. It is a psalm of praise to God for His excellent greatness. He is great because of His concern for the needy, the oppressed, and the forgotten. This study points out two things: God's admonition to unjust judges (Psalm 82), and God's justice (Psalm 113:5-9).

GOD'S ADMONITION TO UNJUST JUDGES (PSALM 82)

Psalm 82 is a reminder to all of those in positions of authority to be just and fair in the exercise of their power and influence. God Himself according to the judgment they render on others will judge "Judges." This psalm has as its basis two important facts. First that God sets the standard by which all others must exercise their judgments. Second, that the problem of injustice and inequality is a reality in the world.

The narrator of this psalm has been privileged to observe the convening of God's heavenly council. He immediately witnesses God verbally chastising members of the heavenly council for their dishonesty and wicked judgments in the world. They practiced partiality and discrimination in relationship to their verdicts.

This passage reveals that nothing escapes God's piercing eyesight. Their actions indict them. The antidote to their previous acts of injustice is to recall their verdicts. God issues to them the double imperative "to provide justice" and "rescue the weak." They must vindicate the forsaken, elevate the oppressed and outcast, and deliver the weak and destitute from the wicked.

Verses 5-9 shift the scene to explain the great deficit of these condoners of injustice. They lack knowledge, understanding, and enlightenment. Because of their multiple deficits, the parts of the earth given to their charge have been seriously mismanaged. Therefore, God Himself judges these ungodly gods. The use of the emphatic "I" leaves no doubt that God Almighty is displeased with them. They exist because of Him, and their failure to execute His standard of justice and equality inaugurates His devastating judgment of mortal death upon them.

Verse 8 is the reply of the worshipers who have seen this scene play out. They respond by calling upon God to exercise His righteous judgment. The earth and the nations of the earth belong to Him. They declare it is not only God's sovereign right to judge but imply that only God will do so fairly.

GOD'S JUSTICE
(PSALM 113:5-9)

The scene of the study shifts to the 113th Psalm. After calling for continuous praise to the Lord, the writer declares God's incomparable glory, power, and concern for humanity. The hymn signifies God as the one who elevates the down trodden, poor, and needy. Those who the affluent chose to forget God acknowledges. He reverses their status from residence in the dust and ashes and places them on equal footing with those who chose to ignore them.

Furthermore in verse 9 He raises the status of women. In Old Testament times women who passed the normal age of childbirth were considered accursed and an embarrassment to their husbands. It attests that God does the impossible for those that were barren become fruitful bearing children. The poet closes this psalm the way he began it with a call to praise the Lord.

SUMMARY

We live in a world full of inequalities and injustice. Many in our society and world are neglected and unfortunate, poor, disenfranchised, and underprivileged. The question for many is not who can afford to wear name brand tennis shoes or designer jeans, but "When will I eat again?" The resources of our world are vast and plentiful; God made it that way. Yet not all share these resources equally because of unfair distribution, the desire to make a profit, and human indifferences. Many people are despised because of the pigmentation of their skin, place of residence, physical appearance, family background, economic condition, and a host of other things. Some youth are not accepted because they do not fit the profile of the group. The justice that God demands is that we as Christians do not misjudge and mistreat people based upon the exterior. All persons are valuable to God and should be accepted by us. We must demand that all people have equal access to the resources of society that will enrich their lives. When we fail to voice our opposition to society's inequities, then we prohibit ourselves from fully understanding, experiencing, and distributing the love of God. It is the gift of God that we should be one another's keeper and vanguard, that all people fully experience His omnipotent love. We must also strive for the standard of God to measure our peers and more importantly to evaluate ourselves. As those who are blessed to be in God's love net, we must share this love in such a way that we actively demonstrate and campaign for justice for all.

DISCUSSION QUESTIONS

1. Why does God chastise the heavenly council He convenes?

2. What does this lesson teach us about God?

3. Why does the poet of Psalm 113 begin and end his song with praise to God?

4. Why does God engage Himself in human affairs?

5. Detail the Christian and human responsibility to be our "brothers' and sisters' keeper."

6. Discuss what divine and social justice mean in terms of the love net.

CHAPTER TWELVE
God Demands a Just Society

— Jeremiah 22:13-17, 21-23 —

"Take Good Care of One Another"

I spoke to you in your prosperity, but you said, "I will not listen." (Jeremiah 22:21)

INTRODUCTION

The old cliché, treat people as you desire to be treated, is the root of this passage. God abhors the establishing of hierarchies that enshrine the rich and powerful with privileges and opportunities at the expense of the poor and unfortunate. He calls humanity to acknowledge its common brotherhood as equal members of God's human creation. This text points out God's desire for human beings to live in peace and harmony with one another. His will is that we acknowledge our common heritage as His children and thus share the produce of the one earth upon which we live. Failure to share the abundant resources that He has given results in the execution of His righteous judgment upon us.

There exists within certain segments of humanity the tendency to conceive of itself as being the "apple of God's eye." That is to say that groups of human beings sometimes seek to elevate themselves to a higher level over others, and in the process of this self-elevation, they abuse the God-given rights of others. In the pericope of Scripture before us God indicts the rich and politically powerful monarch and officials of Judah as the "blood leeches" of their day. They reverse the "Robin Hood trend" by taking from the poor for themselves. They did to their Jewish subjects materially what King David did to Uriah in relationship to David taking Uriah's wife, Bathsheba, for himself (2 Samuel 11-12). This study has four main parts. First, it examines God's judgment of woe for human rights abuses (vv. 13-14); second, the king is forced to examine the legacy of Josiah as a person of social justice (vv. 15-16); third, He indicts them for their abuses and disregard for civil rights (v. 17); and finally the announcement of the judgment of God on Jehoiakim for his social infractions (vv. 21-22).

GOD'S JUDGMENT OF WOE FOR HUMAN RIGHTS ABUSE (JEREMIAH 22:13-14)

The events in this text occurs under the rise of Egyptian imperialism as Egypt, Assyrian, and Babylon play "Russian Roulette" in terms of their fight for political, economic, and military domination of Asia Minor. At this time Egypt has the upper hand and demonstrates it by replacing Jehoiahaz with Jehoiakim. Unconcerned about the condition of his people, the new king adopts a policy of self-indulgence and greed. He shows his political immaturity as he erects elaborate structures "on the backs" of those who are least able to support them. Egypt already overly taxed the people as Judah had come under Egyptian rule and was basically a colony of Egypt. Now to make matters worse Jehoiakim, one of their own, rapes them even more with his vision of self-aggrandizement. God condemns the social atrocities of Jehoiakim and similar inhuman infractions in our day as well.

The entire pericope of Scripture is addressed to Jehoiakim. His record of human right abuse gained the attention of God. This passage is reminiscent of Exodus 2-3, known more specifically as the call of Moses to the prophetic ministry. In Exodus God hears, observes, knows the cry of Hebrew oppression and declares that He will descend His throne in heaven to answer and correct the situation. God immediately sends

Moses to proclaim His judgment against human injustice. The word to Pharaoh is "Let my people go!" Words of warning are followed by decisive action. Egypt suffers ten debilitating plagues and total destruction of their military superiority in their defeat at the Red Sea for their failure to heed God's warning. A similar word of warning is issued here against Jehoiakim. The first indication that this is a warning and a sin that the vassal king should run away from comes in the "woe" given in verse 13. God has observed and judged Jehoiakim's social injustice. At a time when the nation's resources should have gone to help alleviate the people's oppression and suffering from repeated colonization, Jehoiakim helps himself to the nation's coffers, further oppressing the people. This woe is directed to the one responsible for sparing no expense to build an elaborate palace at the expense of the people. To make matters worse Jehoiakim has made slaves out of the workers by refusing to pay them wages. He abused the authority of his office and effectively suck the life out of his workers. The woe of verse 13 is again implied in verse 14, woe to him who says that I will build a monumental chamber. The prophet Jeremiah, however, is not impressed with Jehoiakim's extremity, and more importantly neither is God. The next sections reveals God's displeasure and His attempt to call him to return to the righteous pattern set by his father Josiah.

JEHOIAKIM FORCED TO EXAMINE THE RIGHTEOUS PATTERN SET BY HIS FATHER (JEREMIAH 22:15-16)

Jeremiah offers a set of contrasts between Jehoiakim and his father Josiah to drive his point home. The prophet points out that contrary to Jehoiakim's lavishness, Josiah's kingly need had been met without the use of oppressive economic maneuvers. The text identifies Jehoiakim as the culprit in this comparison. "Your father enjoyed the benefits of royalty yet he maintained justice and righteousness and simultaneously expressed concern for the poor and needy." The writer asks the most prevalent interrogative in the text, "Was this not knowing me?" says the Lord. The implication is that the one who does justice and is an advocate of the poor and needy is the one who has an intimate relationship with God. Evidence that we are in God's divine love net comes in how we treat others, primarily the unfortunate among us. This text recalls Jesus' identification with the poor and the oppressed in Matthews parable of the nations in Matthew 25:40. He said, "Just as you did it to one of the least of these who are members of my family, you did it to me" (NRSV). Knowing God as expressed by Josiah's actions is what made things well with Josiah. God provided for him, and the implication is also made that he found a level of satisfaction in doing what he knew to be right. The prophet lays Josiah's pattern of justice, righteousness, and concern for the poor and needy before Jehoiakim as if to make a final plea with him to follow his father's example or face the justice of God.

JEHOIAKIM INDICTED FOR SOCIAL INFRACTIONS (JEREMIAH 22:17)

Verse 17 moves from the implicit to the explicit. Jehoiakim is indicted for his civil and human rights abuses. The use of "yet" serves not only as a transition, but it also refers to the king's failure to please God. His persistence in social injustice lands him in the divine court. The indictment is also a summons for the king to respond to. His inner disposition has been read by God and announced as "covetousness," as sinfully wanting and desiring that which rightfully belonged to others. Furthermore, the king is guilty of shedding innocent blood, practicing oppression, and violence. God has observed Jehoiakim's atrocities against his own people and has pronounced him guilty. This verse reminds us that God governs those who govern. Political leaders do not have a blank check or unlimited power to do whatever they so desire. They are responsible to govern with justice and human concern. Jehoiakim, however, governed with an eye toward his own political self-aggrandizement. He must answer to God for his injustice and oppression.

FINAL ANNOUNCEMENT OF GOD'S JUDGMENT ON JEHOIAKIM (JEREMIAH 22:21-23)

These verses illustrate the discontentment of God with Jehoiakim's failure to listen to God. God had spoken to the king, but to no avail. Jehoiakim insisted on doing things to appease himself. His interest was purely for the gratification of self. Therefore he did not listen to God. The failure to listen as depicted in this text is the failure to obey God. Listening carries with it more than the connotation of mere hearing as to recognize and distinguish sounds and information. Listening is hearing and obeying the voice of God as the transmittance of His purpose and of His good and perfect will for human life. In this situation the voice of God fell on deaf ears as well as on a stubborn heart. Jehoiakim had no intent to listen to the voice of God. As a consequence of his refusal to hearken to God, Jehoiakim brings on himself the judgment of God. The final two verses describe the extent of this judgment and its severity. Two things are involved here. First it shows that the effect of sin is pervasive and real. Captivity and pain was the result of their sin. Second it shows that regardless of our positions of political power that God, the sovereign Lord of human history, has the final word. Jehoiakim's insistence on exercising his own will proved detrimental not only to himself but to his nation as well. This passage is a real indication that our sin adversely affects others as well as ourselves. The nation would be taken into captivity and would lose its political prestige and position. The neighboring nations of Egypt, Assyria, and Babylon would continually oppress her as a consequence of Judah oppressing her own. It was to be a case of Judah reaping what she had sown, oppression for oppression. This passage shows God reversing the table of fortune on Jehoiakim. Judah's captivity would be the wages of his sinful employment. Their captivity would be accompanied by distress, agony, and excruciating pain. Jeremiah compares Judah's pain with that of a woman in labor. These pains are naturally sharp and intense. They penetrate the very essence of one's being. The meaning of these types of pain as ascribed to Judah is that her captivity would be a severe blow and utterly devastating to the selfish and oppressive king and indifferent nation. The price of the young king's rebellion against God was complete destruction.

SUMMARY

This text shows that human oppression, social, economic, political, religious, or otherwise, does not escape the judgment of God. God ordained humanity to live in brotherhood. He has made us our brothers' and sisters' keepers (Genesis 4). Jehoiakim failed to realize this very important principle. His failure to listen and recant his sins of oppression and violence earned him the right to be judged by Him who is the Father and "Judge" of all humanity. His judgment brought to an end the stubborn resistance of a king who sought alliances with other nations in an attempt to maintain his political entourage. The price he paid for his selfish maneuvers was a costly one, one that seventy years in captivity and years of physical rebuilding could not repay.

This text also illustrates how humanity refuses to listen to the voice of God. Jehoiakim, bent on his own self-aggrandizement, desired only to further his political situation. The choice to follow God means to go against oneself, something Jehoiakim was not willing to do. However, the love of God warns him continuously of his sin and calls him to return to the way of God. The king's refusal to listen by way of obedience led to his destruction and to the destruction of his people. Just as he oppressed his own people, other nations would oppress him. God brings about a reversal of fortune.

Two real points are important to contemporary human beings. First it points out that we must answer to God for the things that we say and do and think. Second it illustrates that God loves all human beings and that He will not stand for the erection of false hierarchical barriers between them. There is even a third point. God will be sure that we reap what we sow. Jehoiakim disregarded God's law of human equality and oppressed his own people. He regarded others as inhuman pawns to serve his lavish desires. God judged him guilty and promised slavery, oppression, and hardship as his punishment. What he did to others he reaped for him. Being caught in God's divine love net means we are prohibited from making ourselves superior at the demise and expense of others.

DISCUSSION QUESTIONS

1. Why did Israel's leaders defy God and develop political alliances with their neighbors?

2. How does developing such alliances compromise our relationship with God?

3. What does the scriptural text teach about reversals?

4. What does God do when we disregard His love for us?

5. What does God's law of human equality say about the concept of being caught in the love net?

CHAPTER THIRTEEN

We Are the Lord's

— Romans 14:1-13 —

"Together in God's Love Net?"

Let us therefore no longer pass judgment on one another, but resolve instead never to put a stumbling block or hindrance in the way of another. (Roman 14:13, NRSV)

INTRODUCTION

Paul concludes that love was the one defining characteristic that exemplified the quality of life the Christian must maintain. In this passage Paul continues to stress the practical aspect of Christian living; however, in a different context. He points out that the existence of Christians and Christian communities do not erase individual preferences or differences. Paul is arguing, however, for a better way to approach differences that leaves the personal dignity of persons intact and becomes a bridge to building successful relationships. The study is set within the context of preferences of eating meat sacrificed to idols and the observance of special events, but its main thrust is to honor human diversity and to use the love of God as the base for handling potential conflict.

This lesson has three parts (all who come to God are welcomed by Him (vv. 1-4), Christ is Lord, therefore we should must not make too much of individual preferences (vv. 5-9), and God is the judge of all (vv. 10-13). Taken together, these three aspects of the text point to the greatness of God's love and the wonderful possibilities that are ours because of it.

ALL WHO COME TO GOD ARE WELCOMED BY HIM (ROMANS 14:1-3)

The question before us is, "How does love reconcile the conflict that comes when two or more persons believe something differently about the same thing?" How does love work to resolve specific issues that we feel deeply about without giving up the principles upon which our lives are built? Paul notes three things in these verses that are of significant importance. In the latter part of verse 3 he notes, "God has received the person who is weak in the faith." In fact this verse serves as a reminder that God has received us like He has received our fellow Christians who are weak in the faith.

Our common acceptance by God should be the major reason for our accepting them. It is the love net concept. Paul is dealing with conflict that arose among Christians about whether or not they should eat meat that had been offered up previously to idols. Should they eat contaminated food? (See 1 Cor. 8-10, and Mark 7:14-23) The point of Paul's exposition here is to stress that we are to refrain from judging others and must not rush to condemn them because they differ from us. They are answerable only to God in matters of following their conscience.

Paul emphasizes that one of the important Christian characteristics is love. Love has the ability to be tolerant. Love recognizes that we grow and develop at different rates and levels. Rather than condemn Christians who are growing up into the faith, we are to help them primarily by modeling our fuller understanding of the faith. God accepts them where they are, and our love for God should cause us to accept them also. All Christians are servants of the one true God, and God will provide the necessities for them to grow and develop.

CHRIST IS LORD OVER ALL
(ROMANS 14:5-10)

These verses further illustrate by way of example how Christians are to handle diverse opinions. Various influences might work to convince one that one day was better than another. Those who had been reared under Jewish influences might esteem their customs and cultural observations as more important than the days and events honored by their Gentile counterparts. Paul warns them against such a stance. Is he imploring the Roman Christians to do away with their heritage? Of course not! Paul is asserting that one person's convictions are equally important as the next person's. If there is a desire to please God, then God will bring those weak in the faith to a more perfect understanding of their faith. Thus mature Christians must be careful not to indulge in legalism, which makes the abstention from certain food and observance of special events more important than the recognition that Jesus Christ is Lord and has by faith justified us before God. Conforming to the will of God is the one duty of the Christian.

GOD ALONE JUDGES
(ROMANS 14:10-13)

Paul concludes this section by pointing out a common sin made by all people including people of the faith, human pride. Because we deem ourselves to be righteous, often we look upon others with disdain, especially those who have not conformed to our method of doing things. Paul corrects this misconception of religion in these verses. Those who differ with us in terms of eating certain foods and observing certain events are not to be judged or incur our ridicule. They are our brothers and sisters, not our servants. Nor are we their "Lords." Paul emphasizes the concept of family. Then he adds with a voice of clarity that all human and cosmic judgment is the absolute prerogative of the sovereign God. All persons including us will come under the judgment of God and will either praise or confess (or both) that Jesus Christ is Lord. Paul notes that the right to judge belongs to God alone. We should be slow to judge and since we are all sinners and come short of the glory of God quick to forgive. Therefore, those who are strong in the faith must accept developing Christians where they are and not carelessly place obstacles in their way that would prevent them from growing up into the faith. Christian love compels those strong in the faith to nurture and care for those who are not now where we are.

SUMMARY

Judgment belongs to God. He judges from the standpoint of complete knowledge because He knows the heart. Paul's point in this passage of Scripture is to encourage Christians to take into account one another's background and culture before they views others' practice as sinful. Because others are not where we are is no reason to condemn them or even to elevate ourselves above them. The rightful action is to exemplify a disposition of love, tolerance, and patience with those who are not as strong in the faith as we. He urges Christians to model their faith by showing love to those who are yet on the way to maturity. Christians must be careful at this point lest they cut off relationships with those who do not possess the gifts and talents they possess or the same beliefs. The better response is to continue to fellowship with them. Model your faith, and take opportunities that God gives you to tell them why you believe as you do. Christians must not forget to pray for those who have an immature concept of the faith. We can best catch others in the divine love net by exemplifying his love in our daily lives.

DISCUSSION QUESTIONS

1. What does Paul mean by the term "weak" in the faith?

2. What are some contemporary issues that can lead to mis-understanding among Christians?

3. Why did Paul urge Christians who had a better concept or understanding of Christianity to refrain from judging other Christians?

4. What are some of the things you can do to help assure the growth and development of maturing Christians?

5. How can I become less judgmental of others?

CHAPTER FOURTEEN

Heirs with Christ

— Galatians 3:6-9, 23—4:7 —

"God's Blended Family"

In Christ Jesus you are all children of God through faith. (Galatians 3:26, NRSV)

INTRODUCTION

This study contains two important points. First, it points out that God accepts believers by faith. Second, it emphasizes that all persons who have been baptized into Christ are members of the family of God and as such are heirs to His promise of salvation. This means that Christians or believers of all generations and from various cultures have equal access to the kingdom of God and to the presence of the Holy Spirit. Their common point is their faith in Jesus Christ. They are effectively caught in God's love net and securely tied to Him and one another by their faith in Jesus Christ.

GOD ACCEPTS BELIEVERS BY FAITH
(GALATIANS 3:6-9)

When I was a boy there was an old adage that said, "Like father like son." It meant that the son could not help but be like or resemble his father. Another old saying went, "Chip off the old block doesn't fall far." This meant that the chip could not be radically different from the block from which it came. This is precisely the point Paul uses to refute the Judaizers' claim that they are heirs of God through Abraham because they ascribe to Abraham keeping of the Law of Moses. (See Gen. 12-17)

Paul refutes their argument by using the same scripture (Gen. 12-17) they used as his basis to deny their claim to be heirs or children of Abraham. Paul agrees with them that Abraham was accepted or justified by God. But he disagrees with them as to the method of his justification. Paul contends that Abraham's obedience in keeping the law was a result of his faith, not his works. Rather than works it was Abraham's faith expressed as trusting response to God's call which God evaluated as righteous. Having then established Abraham as a person of faith, Paul emphasizes that it is persons of similar faith who are children of Abraham. Therefore, because the Judaizers sought to minimize the necessity of faith and maximize keeping the law (works), they were not children of Abraham.

For Paul, faith, the trusting response to God's initiative and call, is the determining characteristic that distinguishes the children of Abraham, irrespective of biological or cultural relationships. Paul points out that physical descent from Abraham is not a passport to salvation. Biological ties as well as cultural identification were irrelevant. The true children of Abraham are those who like Abraham exercise faith in God and are faithful to God. They are those who believe God's promises and entrust themselves to His love and mercy. Paul argues that God accepted Abraham solely because he surrendered his life to God's promise. Thus he is the father of all who believe whether they are Gentile or Jew.

Since Abraham was justified by faith, Gentiles are justified in Abraham because all nations will be blessed in connection with Abraham (Gen. 18:8). Therefore since Gentiles are justified in Abraham's promise, they must be justified, as Abraham was, by faith, not works of the law.

ALL BELIEVERS ARE MEMBERS OF "THE FAMILY OF GOD" (GALATIANS 3:23—4:7)

In these verses Paul has two things in mind: the purpose and function of the law, and the function of God's promise in history. In pointing out these two things he is seeking to establish a new concept for believers—as members of the "Family of God." In doing so he eliminates the idea of Jewish privileges and distinctions as ultimate in God's plan of salvation. Biological ties and adherence to rituals as the guiding principles of life are not accepted by God to gain His meritorious favor. Indeed the only way one can be accepted by God is by being justified in Jesus Christ.

For Paul the function of the law was to reveal sin. It was never designed to bring "saving life." The Jewish people had mistakenly and selfishly elevated the "Law of Moses" to a position that God did not intend. They elevated the law to a position which God used to redeem His people. "No!" Paul declared. The law is not intended to bring life. Its purpose is to reveal sin. Therefore the Judaizers erred in demanding the Christians at Galatia to follow it in order to be accepted by God. Paul continues by pointing out that the law not only reveals Israel's sinfulness, but it imprisoned her as well. It was a judging instrument for the people of God so they could learn that certain behavior was contrary to the will of God. It could only show them where they were. In other words the law was a tool designed to prepare people for the coming of the apex of God's plan of salvation. It was never designed to be an end in itself. It was a temporal measure at best. It served three purposes: It revealed human sinfulness and the inability to deal with it; it was to lead them to Christ and prepare them for renewed fellowship with God; and it served as a guide to understanding moral principles.

Thus since faith has come, the era of the law is obsolete. No longer are believers under a strict moral disciplinarian, but by faith they are children of God in Jesus Christ. The era of Christ eclipses the era of Moses because the era of Christ is the climax of God's promise to Abraham. Paul argues the law had a limited purpose, and this limited purpose was for a limited time, until Christ had come. So once faith came, the law which could not save could no longer condemn.

Paul argues that the Judaizers are wrong (and so are those Galatians who followed them) because they do not understand why God gave the law. They do not know that it was designed to turn Israel's bad behavior into transgression of God's law. Nor do they know that it was given only for a short period. Consequently they do not know that everything for salvation and acceptance by God is established in Abraham (his faith). Consequently they do not know that by imposing the law after Christ and equivocating it with Christ is a gross step backward to a previous era of slavery and condemnation. They are living a "horse and buggy" lifestyle in the jet age. They are living in the age of the typewriter, rather in the age of the computer. They do not understand the progressive revelation of God about Himself beginning with Abraham to Moses until Christ. (Romans 6:11-14; 7:7-13; 11:25-32; 2 Cor. 3:7-18; Phil. 3:2-11)

In 3:25—4:7 Paul begins to develop the idea that all who have faith are heir of the promise God made to Abraham. Again he chastises the Judaizers for re-invoking the law. The law was (mis)used by the Jewish people not only to show their "righteousness, but also to separate themselves from ("dirty and sinful") Gentiles. Paul in these verses repudiates all types of racial, class, and social prejudice and sexual discrimination based upon the new solidarity in Christ Jesus. In verse 29 he connects the passage back to verses 6-9 by pointing out Abraham's offspring as those who belong to Christ. Abraham received a promise, and they would be heirs of it by exercising faith in Jesus Christ.

SUMMARY

Jesus Christ removed the barriers that separated people from God and one another. Faith in Him makes Christians into one community of faith (hence, the love net). Therefore we are brothers and sisters in the faith. This faith does not erase the fact that we come from different places, go to school in different locations, and have our own peculiarities. What it does say is that we realize that God is the Father and creator of all people, and that our faith in His Son Jesus Christ unites us in a way that overcomes all of our difference. As members of the same family—the "Family of God—we desire others to come to know of His loving grace. We proclaim His Word in an effort to extend His love to others so that others may find joy, fulfillment, and their purpose in life. We possess a great opportunity to extend this wonderful family by exhibiting in our lives the love of God. We must carry the message that one does not have to join a gang, participate in premarital or extra-marital sex, resort to drugs or prostitution or promiscuity to feel loved and accepted. Neither do they have to give up on life by committing suicide. Christians can carry the message to others who feel depressed and rejected, "You are loved by God and by us."

DISCUSSION QUESTIONS

1. How was Abraham made righteous before God?

2. How are believers like Abraham or made into children of Abraham?

3. What happened to the law when Christ came?

4. How does the coming and accepting of Christ work to break down barriers between people?

5. What does the term the "Family of God" mean?

6. How does the concept of the love net relate to understanding the image of the "Family of God?"

Section IV

LIVING IN
HOPE AND TRUST

CHAPTER FIFTEEN

The Lord, Our Keeper

— Psalms 23; 121 —

"Someone to Watch Over Me"

I lift up my eyes to the hills—from where will my help come? My help comes from the Lord, who made heaven and earth. (Psalm 121:1-2, NRSV)

INTRODUCTION

These two psalms are psalms of trust in God. They express a deep abiding faith and confidence in the ability and willingness of God to protect, care, and nurture. They are solid affirmations gleaned from the psalmist's past experience with God. They are both known for their picturesque imagery that defines God's unchanging love and eternal presence as the foundation of individual security and stability. Psalm 23 identifies itself as a "Psalm of David" while Psalm 121 is one of 15 psalms called "Pilgrim Psalms." Pilgrims who journeyed to and from Jerusalem for the feasts probably sang them. The dates of these two poetic expositions cannot be stated precisely, nor is it extremely important to do so because the messages they give transcend both time and place. These psalms are universal expressions of a convicted heart and the firm affirmation of God's ability to keep those who put their trust in Him. Coupled together they produce a solid testimony of faith that the psalmist used in worship to describe who God is and what God does. This study has three parts: the Good Shepherd (Psalm 23:1-4), God as the Good and Gracious Host (vv. 5-6), and God the Great Keeper (Psalm 121:1-8).

GOD THE GOOD SHEPHERD
(PSALM 23:1-4)

The writer begins this psalm by conjecturing a softer and more humane image of God without distorting any of His divine characteristics. The Lord of life, the Creator, Sustainer, and Redeemer of the universe are set in a personal picturesque image of a caring Shepherd. And since it is the Lord (Yahweh) who is his "Shepherd," all of his needs are abundantly supplied. The poet has no need of anything. By using the metaphor of a "Shepherd" to describe God's care for him, the psalmist emphasizes God's guardianship. This guardianship begins with God supplying the most basic needs of life. From the very beginning of this song, it is God who takes the initiative. But there is an implication that more than the physical is referred to here. Verse 4 stresses the presence of God, which fulfills the writer's other needs, which are not tangible. The psalmist is given peace, his energies are replenished, and none other than God Himself guides him in the ways that are right. God is known for His wonderful acts and will live up to His history as one that cannot and will not change.

The fourth verse wraps up this section as it illustrates the power of God, which relieves him of all fear of harm, whether it be from the lurking of death or some other evil foe. God is present with him even as he walks into unknown places that may be dangerous. The rod was a stout club used to beat those who endangered the sheep, while the staff was a tool used to guide the sheep through the darkness of night and other distractions. This verse paints a picture of tender love and care.

GOD AS THE GOOD AND GRACIOUS HOST
(PSALM 23:5-6)

In this section the psalmist builds on the preceding verses that established God as the good gracious host. To emphasize this point he changes the metaphor. Now God is the good and gracious provider whose love is seen in His position as host of a great "get together." This God knows the psalmist personally. The psalmist is His special guest and prepares for him the best table in the presence of the psalmist's persecutors. As in the case of the lurking of death or some hidden foe in verse 4, the writer is protected by the presence of such a host. The psalmist is singled out and honored by the host of the feast. The poet is overwhelmed and beams with joy over the bounty of God. God who has no reason to be so loving and hospitable is. It is the reason he can speak affirmatively of the unchanging love of God as his companion for life. He will always be a permanent guest in God's house.

GOD THE GOOD KEEPER
(PSALM 121)

The emphasis on the presence of God and on His ability to protect and comfort the poet of Psalm 23 has already established the thematic link it has with Psalm 121. This link is immediately established in response to the poet's question about the source of his help. As indicated earlier in the introduction, Psalm 121 is a psalm of trust from the "Pilgrim Collection." It is highly probable that this psalm was recorded testimony and dialogue between a priest or spiritual leader and his group as they traveled to and from Jerusalem. Having to camp along the way to their destination, this group subjected itself to ambush and other remote dangers, including the elements of nature. It is out of this context that the question to determine the source of his help emerges.

The remainder of the psalm is a comprehensive response to one of life's most important questions. His question really asks, when and how soon will my help arrive? God's help is needed now. These verses state that God is his help and that God is coming to the rescue. No power or obstacle can prevent His arrival. God's coming will not be prevented because

God is not inhibited by things that curtail human activity such as the need to sleep or slumber. God is always watchful. He does not doze or nod.

In the background of this psalm is the negative and sublime thought of the poet that maybe God has neglected him. The poet is then reminded that the Lord is his keeper. The Lord is his constant guardian. Thus he remembers he is special to God. God has always protected him from a variety of foes and calamities. Even now God is doing so. Not even the elements can parch his soul for the Lord controls them as well. The answer to the question then is that God, the Creator of all things, is your help. He will keep a watchful eye over you; He will keep you in every pilgrimage or journey you make now and forever. You are safe and secure in His love net.

SUMMARY

This lesson is important because it reminds Christians to whom they belong; they belong to God. There are times in our lives when the lack of a secure and stable environment produces havoc and anxiety for us. The message of these two psalms serves to remind us that God is still in control and nothing can sever believers from His love. They once again are caught securely in His love net. It calls upon Christians to put their trust in God. As a Shepherd cares for the sheep and wards off those who would devour them, God protects and cares for the faithful. They can find in Him a constant source of help and guidance.

DISCUSSION QUESTIONS

1. What is the theme running through Psalm 23 and Psalm 121?

2. What type of psalms are they?

3. What does the change of metaphors in Psalm 23 indicate?

4. What is the major emphasis in Psalm 121?

5. Compare and contrast these two psalms? What are the major points of emphasis that Christians can use to validate their authenticity?

6. Relate the themes or emphases of these two psalms to the love net theological perspective?

CHAPTER SIXTEEN

Hope In God
— Psalm 42:1-6a, 7-10 —
"Don't Lose Hope"

Hope in God; for I shall again praise him, my help and my God. (Psalm 42:11b, NRSV)

INTRODUCTION

Psalm 42 begins the second of five sections or books in the Psaltery. In this section (42-72) the word for God (Elohim) is used much more extensively than Yahweh. This along with the poet being physically separated from the geographical landscape of Jerusalem and from worshipping in the Temple of the Lord in Jerusalem combine to explain his use of the more general term for God and to indicate that the reason for his separation might be related to the Exile. It is probable then that this psalm was composed during the period of Jewish exile in Babylon. At any rate this separation from his once familiar surroundings and from his place of worship of the one true God caused him great distress and anguish.

Originally Psalms 42 and 43 were once a single psalm. This fact is brought out in the common theme of longing for God and in the continuous and recurring refrain. (see 42:5, 11, and 43:5) Furthermore some manuscripts of the Psalms join them into one poem. There are two related points of emphasis in Psalm 42 "His yearning for God's presence" (vv. 1-6a), and "his longing for God in the face of hopelessness" (vv. 7-10). The points suggest that the major theme of the psalmist is to rekindle a disposition of hope and enthusiasm as the platform for living.

His Yearning for God
(Psalm 42:1-6a)

The first part of this psalm is a basic complaint that emphasizes the writer's despair with being physically separated from the place of divine worship. It is a psalm that points to the poet's need for God's presence. This need for God is compared by way of simile to a panting and extremely thirsty deer that desires to be refreshed by the cool streams to replenish itself. The author of this song was a man of deep faith who for some reason had been removed from the Holy City of Jerusalem and worship in the Temple. Worshipping God in the Temple had been a regular and immensely important part of his life. But his separation from the Temple was more than geographic in nature. It was a separation that left him feeling isolated and alone. This isolation was worsened by the taunts of those who jeered at him because of his faith.

Thus, the author expresses his desire to return to the Jerusalem Temple where God's presence was real to him. He longs for God. His soul is parched. His desire for God's presence caused him to reflect on days past and gone that were the apex of his existence. He remembers leading and participating in celebrative and festive processions to the Temple and hearty exultations to the Lord God. These remembrances cause him to catch himself and end his plunge into further despair. It is a time for self-evaluation. Should he continue to shed tears and be grieved by the taunts of those around him? Should the present situation and circumstances defeat him? No! When all else is lost there is yet one thing that remains. Hope in God! (v. 5) He encourages himself to climb out of his pit sorrow on the steps of his hope in God.

Longing for God in the Midst of Hopelessness (Psalm 42:7-10)

But there are times when despair has grown into utter hope-lessness, and try as one might to rid oneself of it depression deepens. This is the situation the psalmist finds himself in. His depression was overwhelming and deeply rooted in his self-pity. As soon as he regains his fortitude he loses it again. The waterfall crashing down from Mount Herman again triggers his memory of his experience with God. It is a memory that re-ignites his trust and confidence and hope. The succession of sorrows that fueled his plunge into deep despair, his separation from his homeland and from Temple worship, the taunts of his peers, he funnels into spiritual resources that provide his deliverance from depression. The gloom and doom of his present predicament are not able to turn him against God or to lose hope in God. In the silence, he finds reason for hope and vows to praise the Lord continuously. The psalmist was finally able to comfort himself the more he concentrated on God's presence with him. He finds strength in the knowledge that whether he is in Jerusalem or not that God's presence and power will envelope him and secured him in the divine love net.

Summary

Situations occur in the lives of Christians that can be overwhelming. A family move across town or to another part of the country, a change of familiar surroundings can be a frightening experience for Christians. The real probability of not fitting in or being different can also magnify feelings of isolation. Coming from a family that cannot afford the name brand clothing or shoes and is living in lower class neighborhoods can increase the frustration. Believers are reminded that God accepts them for whom they are. Relocating to strange or to an unfamiliar neighborhood does not cut them off from the love of God and from the ability to worship Him and seek His face. Life situations change, but throughout these changes God is there for us. Christians are encouraged to collect their sorrows and things that depress them and to use them as steppingstones to climb out of self-sorrow and see that their hope lies not in things but in God. The evidence of being caught in His divine love net is that He is there for you.

DISCUSSION QUESTIONS

1. Why does the poet long for God's presence?

2. What are the circumstances that come together to plunge the author of this poem into despair?

3. What conclusion does he come to about his circumstances and about God's love for him?

4. How can we use the love of God as a point of assurance that God has our back?

5. Why is it essential for us like the psalmist to face our grief, sorrows, and problems with courage and hope?

Chapter Seventeen
Rejection and Mission

— Mark 6:1-13 —

"Mission Accomplished"

And they took offense at him.... So they went out and proclaimed that all should repent. (Mark 6:3b, 12, NRSV).

INTRODUCTION

This passage of Scripture has two sections. The first section emphasizes Jesus' rejection by His hometown (vv. 1-6a), while the second section emphasizes His evangelistic mission and teaching (vv. 6b-13). Taken together, they deal with the concept of how familiarity can factor into unappreciation of one's ministry. The people of Nazareth had heard of the wonderful deeds of Jesus. His fame preceded him. Stories of His power over sickness, storms, and demons (evil spirits) arrived in Nazareth before Jesus returned. Upon Jesus' return, He did not receive a hero's welcome, only more questions about His identity. They deduced He was nothing more than a local boy. Jesus took their rejection of Him, however, as an opportunity to teach His disciples what ministry entails. Not all people will accept them. "Rejection," He points out, "is a real possibility for them." They are called not to success but to faithfulness to the task. He directs them to depend totally on God's provisions and on the generosity of those who respond to their preaching in a positive way. His teachings serve to show us that real ministry lay in human beings that are called to the evangelistic task. They are forewarned that success of their mission lay not in numbers but in faithfulness to the task.

FAMILIARITY BREEDS CONTEMPT
(MARK 6:1-6A)

The age old adage "familiarity breeds contempt" is the point of this passage of Scripture. Jesus is seen strictly as the boy next door whose escapes are dismissed as nothing more than wild exaggeration. In Jewish and Greek culture, the way to fame and acceptance was to have a family background that included nobility or persons of noble character. Name-dropping was a frequent pastime in early Graeco-Roman culture. Having renown ancestors made one's economic and social status easier and made one more acceptable. Class differentiation was a fact of life in ancient Palestine. Unlike in American life where one's "rags to riches" story receives notoriety and becomes the epitome of success, in Jewish culture, one remained fixed in the class wherein one was born. Upward mobility, though possible, was not highly probable in this ancient culture. Jesus, as a member of the labor class (He was a carpenter by trade), did not have sufficient standing for His hometown to expect anything significant from Him. He had humble beginnings and these remained the basis of His public scrutiny and acted as a prohibition for social advancement. It is appropriate to suggest that the people of Nazareth, true to their cultural upbringing, found it difficult to believe that one could rise above one's "serf-like" status in life.

Being a product of Nazareth also led to Jesus' rejection by His hometown. Instead of receiving a hero's welcome, Jesus' arrival in Nazareth was met with outright skepticism and disbelief. Their question is not "Who is this?" But they concluded, "It can't be little Jesus, Mary's boy." Their reference to His family illustrates the belief that they knew Him and His family well. This passage is the most detailed account of Jesus' background for Mark, who unlike Matthew and Luke, does not begin or induce in his Gospel account Jesus' genealogy. Mark's Gospel begins with Jesus' public ministry, so Jesus' ancestry and linkage to David, the most celebrated king of Israel, is apparently not known to the people of Nazareth. For that matter, nor do they care. They have seen Him grow up. They have shared, to some extent, in His upbringing. Mark shows the extent of their acquaintance with Jesus in the naming of His brothers and in establishing the point that His sisters yet reside there. Not to mention that, at this point in His ministry, Jesus' family does not think much of Him (Mark 3).

Clearly disturbed by the less than enthusiastic reception to His return, Jesus responds by recalling the expression that a prophet is never honored by his own people. In this expression, the term "prophet," used in relationship to Himself, clearly places Jesus in the prophetic tradition. Jesus comes within this prophetic tradition to fulfill it. This tradition emphasizes the rejection of the prophet. The people of Nazareth reject Jesus because He is one of them. Again, the irony of the question of Jesus' identity comes up. Whereas the demons, the ones He has come to eradicate, recognize Him as coming from God. The people of Nazareth even dismiss His miraculous work. What will it take for human beings to recognize who Jesus is? What more does Jesus have to do in order to get humanity to express faith in Him? What will it take for humanity to come to a "demon-like" acknowledgement of His divinity? The truth of the matter is that one must come to the point of dismissing one's rigid expectations of Jesus in order to accept Him as Lord and Savior. Three things are important here. First, one must accept His humanity. God chose to save humanity by entering the human frame of reference. This paradox of the Almighty God becoming totally human and coming in humility is the point of the Gospel. Second, this means that our preconceived ideas about what God does and how He relates to humanity must be changed. God is still sovereign, and human redemption is His mission, and therefore, He established it according to His wisdom. We are called to faith in what God has done. Third, Jesus' coming, His message, and His activities all attest to the unity and consistency of God's call and purpose for His life. His caring denoted a life committed to preaching, teaching, and healing. His message of salvation was based on repentance and faith in Him, and His miracles all bring about human wholeness and restoration. Although seen as the most unlikely vehicle to dispense the salvation of God because of His humble beginnings, erroneous expectations about what the Messiah should look like and do, and cultural familiarity, one must come to accept who Jesus is by faith.

As a natural and inevitable consequence of their lack of faith, the flow of divine blessings to them was restricted. The channel of passage, the channel or tunnel of faith, was blocked by their questioning doubt. Two things are important to remember at this point. First, their lack of faith and thus corresponding lack of blessings was not caused by any deficiency in the power and ability of Jesus. Second, it naturally follows that a lack of faith produces a lack of faithful activity. The truth is Jesus could not do any miraculous works there. They did not believe He came from God, so they failed to respond in a positive way to His preaching. They spent too much time finding reasons to doubt Him. Unlike the four men who brought the paralyzed man and even took the initiative of letting him down through a hole they made in the roof of the house where Jesus was preaching, the people of Nazareth expressed little or no desire to have Jesus do anything for them. "How could He do anything for us," they concluded. He had not elevated the status of His own family. The town's people argued among themselves that His local rearing and lack of family prestige was the basis of their rejection of Him. It was inconceivable that anything good could come out of Nazareth, and because of their unbelief, nothing good could come in. Their lack of faith worked as a prohibitive force that resulted in their deficiency. Here was God's offer of salvation standing in their midst, and they outright rejected it. They refused to be caught in God's divine love net.

OPPORTUNITY FOR SUCCESS AND TRAINING IN MINISTRY (MARK 6:6B-13)

The rejection of Jesus in the previous section of this passage serves a dual purpose. First, it provides Jesus the opportunity to turn an apparent failure into success; and second, He uses His rejection as an opportunity to provide essential ministry training to His disciples.

Jesus had the unfavorable option of letting His disappointing hometown reception stifle and discourage Him or use it as an opportunity to grow, to further His ministry. He chose the latter. Verse 6b shows an undeterred Jesus, moving from place to place, from village to village, teaching the truth of God. His ministry did not stop. He did not hesitate or suspend His mission because the hometown crowd did not accept Him. Jesus determined to persevere. He continued to preach, teach, and heal. The rejection would be used for the growth and development of the Christian ministry. It is almost like a campfire setting where Jesus called together His disciples, here called the "Twelve," and in this intimate setting gave them the benefit of His experience. Verse 7 shows Him empowering them to cast out evil spirits that had found residence in their fellow humans. The casting out of the evil spirits is to make room for divine habitation in human beings. Their mission is the restoration of fellowship between God and humanity. Jesus sent them out in pairs and gave them a clear set of instructions of how they should conduct themselves (Numbers 35:30; Deuteronomy 19:15). He sent them out in pairs as a means of supporting one another and as a witness to the proclamation of God's truth to an unbelieving community. They have already witnessed and observed Jesus' actions. They have served as apprentices under Him. Now in this "on-the-job training" campaign, they are to preach His message of repentance, and they are commissioned to exercise demons.

Now Jesus gives these extra instructions to them for the success of their mission. Again, the emphasis is not on numbers but on their faithfulness as not to distract or bring skepticism upon their work. They are not to get involved in any activity that will rob the ministry of its effectiveness. People must not have an excuse to subsist in their sin and in their unbelief. They are to go preaching in the manner of Elijah and John the Baptist, even in the manner of Jesus Himself. The staff must be their only accompaniment. Their call to ministry is not a call to excessive living. They are called to humility. In the previous section, the people of Nazareth refused to accept Jesus because of His humble beginnings. Now Jesus implores the "Twelve" that humility is a condition to the doing of ministry. They are to take nothing with them except the message of repentance and forgiveness, and a staff. It is a sign of their commitment to the task and an expression of their faith and trust in God and in the people of God. The staff brings to mind images of the prophets, most notably Moses, whose staff symbolized the power, presence, and authority of God (Exodus 4:2-5). In the previous section, Jesus places Himself squarely within the prophetic tradition. Informing them that the staff was the only acceptable item for them to carry in their preaching mission is a continuation of this tradition, which underscores God's presence and power in the current generation and for generations to come.

Jesus also instructs them to wear sandals and to accept the hospitality of the people. That is to say, they are not to be opportunists. They are ordered to accept the generosity of those who initially offer accommodations to them without regard for comfort. The physical incentives provided to them as they carry out their mission are always subjective to their mission. Jesus' instructions emphasize to them that nothing must be allowed to interfere with their mission.

In addition, His instructions imply the seriousness and urgency of their mission. Packing only delays them. Hauling excessive baggage creates an additional delay. This situation focuses on the short time Jesus will be with them and the need for them to receive thorough training to carry on His work. The urgency of the mission requires their immediate attention.

This text also informs them what they are to do if their message is ill received. They are to shake the dust from their feet as a sign of God's judgment upon the unbelievers. Valuable time is not to be spent arguing about the truth of the message or their acceptance of it. The people who hear them are yet free to determine their own way. The choice is theirs to make. If they choose to hear and obey, then they will be the recipients of God's blessings, the blessings demonstrated in the healing and forgiveness of the sins of the crippled man, in the exorcisms of the evil spirits, in the restoration to wholeness, and in the renewal of human fellowship with God. On the other hand, if they reject the disciples' message then they will deprive themselves, as did the people in Nazareth, Jesus' hometown, of the wondrous activities of God. The choice to accept or reject their message of repentance and faith is the people's to make. What is important for the "Twelve" is that they carry the message of what God has done for them in sending Jesus Christ. They are to be sure that their message is not besieged by obstacles created by the disciples' desire to be comfortable or otherwise.

Mark affirms that once they received their instructions from Jesus, they obeyed Him and went out preaching repentance, casting out evil spirits, and healing the sick. Mark does not give any hint about the success of their mission, but he tells us they went out in faith.

SUMMARY

Sharing the Christian faith as a minister or layperson can be a difficult chore, especially when one seeks to share the Gospel with family and friends. Sharing the Gospel with those close to you means to exposing yourself to those who know you best. They know where you came from, what you have said and done, past infractions, deeds of imperfection, and other personal tidbits of information that a stranger would not be aware of. Sharing the Gospel opens up the person to ridicule and disbelief because its perfect message relates to the giver and to the receiver of the message. Yet, the Christian message is of such vital importance that Christians are called to take such risks and to expose themselves by preaching God's message of repentance. Christians are not to commit acts that would contradict the truth of their message, however. Moreover, most importantly, Christians must face the possibility of rejection. They are not to be deterred by failure but to use it as an opportunity to grow. Jesus came to throw out God's love net of human salvation, and He has chosen us to share in this great privilege and ministry with Him. The possibility of failure looms great if we expect praise and gratitude from those among us. But the reality of success is our's through a committed faith to accept His love by sharing it with others.

DISCUSSION QUESTIONS

1. Why is rejection important for Christians to consider?

2. How did Jesus deal with rejection by the people of Nazareth?

3. How did Jesus maintain a clear focus on His mission and ministry?

4. What are some of the important things we can learn from these passages of Scripture?

5. How does the concept of the love net factor into Jesus' rejection and subsequent ministry assignment to His disciples?

6. What does the commitment of Jesus do for us who live in contemporary society?

CHAPTER EIGHTEEN

Teach the Wonders of God

— Psalm 78:1-8 —

"Pass It On"

We will tell to the coming generation the glorious deeds of the Lord, and his might, and the wonders that he has done. (Psalm 78:4, NRSV)

INTRODUCTION

This psalm is a psalm of remembrance and instruction. The writer calls upon his readers and hearers to remember the wonderful activities of God and uses this call to remember as an opportunity to instruct them on their disobedience. Verses 1-8, the main focus of our study's main theme, broadcast the great activities of God in the life of Israel.

This psalm was probably composed during the time of the United Monarchy after the construction of the Temple by Solomon. It was used as an instructional tool, and as such is the basis for some scholars categorizing it as a Wisdom Psalm. The emphasis of the first eight verses is to remind the people about the greatness of God in their history. These verses have two points: the admonition to hear the story of God's dealing with Israel (vv. 1-4), and to pass the story on to succeeding generations (vv. 5-8). This psalm focuses on the continuation of the theme of the love net by sharing the Good News of God's love with those He has placed under our care.

ADMONITION TO HEAR THE STORY OF GOD'S DEALINGS WITH ISRAEL
(PSALM 78:1-4)

This psalm begins with a call to worshipers to listen attentively to the words of the psalmist. He recounts to them things they have heard before. The things he will share with them are to be shared with those of succeeding generations. The purpose of this instruction is to cause them to observe the magnificence of God. The key verse calls upon them to tell, to proclaim the glorious deeds of the Lord. How often we fail to teach our children and youth our heritage and help them to gain a firm spiritual grounding. They need the strong foundation of God's Word to solidify them so that when their time of testing comes they will be able to stand and conquer. The psalmist understands this and calls upon worshipers to root themselves in the historical goodness and mercy of a true and living God. Their very being and essence is rooted in God. It is He who has created, sustained, and redeemed them. In Psalm 46, the psalmist recounts, God is a very present help in time of trouble. Young believers need to know God, for the psalmist assures us that troubled times will surely come. When they do come, they need to be firmly entrenched and secured in His love net.

PASS IT ON
(PSALM 78: 5-8)

Verses 5-8 form a unit, which emphasizes the responsibility of the hearers (and readers) to pass on the message of God's wonderful acts to their children of succeeding generations. It is a command to teach the young about their religious heritage. Just what is this message? It is the message of the historical activities of God in their lives. God established a relationship with Israel before she was a nation and took care of her. He continued to care for and protect her as she developed. He gave the law as a tool to guide her life and instruct her in the way of God. These teachings were to be passed on to the children who were to pass them on as well. There is a purpose for passing on this information. Notice verses 7-8. The purpose is that they might not forget and set their hope in the Lord. There is an old adage, "You can't teach an old dog new tricks." This adage applies to this topic of discussion. In appealing to worshipers to pass on the wonderful, glorious deeds of God, the psalmist contrasts the young receptive heart over against those who were stubborn and rebellious, who insisted on doing things their own way. The reason for this stubbornness lay in the fact that they did not set their hearts right with God. They had grown accustomed to the way things had been done before. Therefore their spirit was one of unfaithfulness to God. By passing this message on to children and youth, there was hope they would not be resistant to God as were their forefathers.

SUMMARY

The people of Israel were instructed to teach their children about their religious heritage. Often in our contemporary society we neglect to pass on to our children, family, and community our Christian heritage. Children and youth need the stability and security of their past to help them identify and define and know who they are. They need to know their spiritual roots. They must be taught that the root of their life is God and that God has been and is actively working on their behalf.

Passing on the Good News and gracious teachings about God will help them to remain open and responsive to God and to doing God's will. Feeding the mind and heart while they are young will help establish our children and encourage their full development as people, and put them on the sure path that leads to success. Passing on the goodness of God's love, His truth, and divine grace affords us an opportunity to secure our young in the divine love net. By doing so, we secure them and ourselves in the divine love net and make human salvation truly a "Family Affair."

DISCUSSION QUESTIONS

1. What is the main objective of this psalm?

2. Why are the first eight verses important for accomplishing this objective?

3. Why does the psalmist encourage his hearers to listen attentively?

4. Why is it important to pass on our heritage to our young?

5. Discuss the ramifications of the failure to pass on the Christian heritage to our youth.

6. How can adults incorporate children and youth in their Christian traditions?

About the Author

Bernard Williams is a native of Nashville, Tennessee. He has pastored churches in Tennessee and Florida. He is a graduate of the University of Tennessee, Knoxville, and the Southern Baptist Theological Seminary in Louisville, Kentucky. Dr. Williams is a great proponent of small group Bible study and serves as a teacher in Christian education. He also holds numerous revivals, conferences, workshops, and seminars.

REFERENCES

Akin, Daniel L. 1, 2, 3 John. *(New American Commentary)*. Broadman & Holman, Nashville, 2001.

Crim, Keith R. and George A. Buttrick. *The Interpreter's Dictionary of the Bible.* Abingdon Press, Nashville, 1976.

Culpepper, Alan R. *Anatomy of the Fourth Gospel: A Study in Literary Design.* Fortress Press, Minneapolis, 1987.

Elwell, Walter A., ed. *Baker Theological Dictionary of the Bible.* Baker Book House Company, Grand Rapids, 2001.

Felder, Cain Hope, ed. *Stony the Road We Trod: African American Biblical Interpretation.* Augsburg Fortress Publishers, Minneapolis, 1991.

Keck, Leander E., ed. *The New Interpreter's Bible: A Commentary in Twelve Volumes.* Abingdon Press, Nashville, 2004.

Gane, Ron, ed. *The NIV Application Commentary.* Zondervan Publishing Company, Grand Rapids, 2004.

Ogilvie, Lloyd J., ed. *The Preacher's Commentary: Old Testament Set.* Thomas Nelson Publishers, Nashville, 2004

Unger, Merrill. *Unger's Bible Handbook.* Moody Press, Chicago, 1992.

Vine, W.E. and Merrill F. Unger. *Vine's Complete Expository Dictionary of Old and New Testament Words: With Topical Index.* Thomas Nelson Publishers, Nashville, 1996.